THE STORY OF A BATTALION.

THE
STORY OF A BATTALION

BY

W. DEVINE

DRAWINGS AND MAPS BY DARYL LINDSAY
(Official Artist with the A.I.F.)

The Naval & Military Press Ltd

Published by
The Naval & Military Press Ltd
5 Riverside, Brambleside, Bellbrook
Industrial Estate, Uckfield, East Sussex,
TN22 1QQ England
Tel: +44 (0) 1825 749494
Fax: +44 (0) 1825 765701
www.naval-military-press.com
www.military-genealogy.com
www.militarymaproom.com

In reprinting in facsimile from the original, any imperfections are inevitably reproduced and the quality may fall short of modern type and cartographic standards.

Dedicated
TO
THOSE WHO LIVED THIS BOOK
THE MEN OF MY BRIGADE

CONTENTS.

	Page
FOREWORD	xi
Chapter 1.—FORMATION OF THE BATTALION	1
Chapter 2.—THE MARCH TO SERAPEUM	6
Chapter 3.—TRAINING FOR FRANCE	12
Chapter 4.—IN FRANCE	19
Chapter 5.—LA SOMME	27
Chapter 6.—POZIERES RIDGE	35
Chapter 7.—POZIERES RIDGE—THE WINDMILL	44
Chapter 8.—POZIERES RIDGE—MOUQUET FARM	51
Chapter 9.—IN FLANDERS	58
Chapter 10.—THE WINTER OF 1916-17	63
Chapter 11.—BULLECOURT	71
Chapter 12.—" THE COLONEL "	80
Chapter 13.—BRIGHTER DAYS	87
Chapter 14.—PASSCHENDAELE	95
Chapter 15.—THE BATTALION'S SPELL	101
Chapter 16.—METEREN TO THE AMIENS ROAD	108
Chapter 17.—THE DEFENCE OF AMIENS	115
Chapter 18.—MONUMENT WOOD	128
Chapter 19.—THE STRAIN LIGHTENS	131
Chapter 20.—TOWARDS THE EAST	136
Chapter 21.—THE BATTALION'S LAST ENGAGEMENT	144
Chapter 22.—THE DAYS OF THE ARMISTICE.	153
Appendix 1.—GENERAL BIRDWOOD'S MESSAGE TO 48TH BATTALION	159
Appendix 2.—BATTALION'S ROLL OF HONOUR	160
Appendix 3.—BATTALION'S HONOURS AND AWARDS	178

LIST OF ILLUSTRATIONS.

" They were for the most part of the country . . . . . they were not a kid-glove lot of men . . . . "

Facing page 4

" . . . . these men came to the desert as clumsy novices . . . . And the desert had no pity on them."

Facing page 8

" The Australian soldier is an adaptable being . . . . At night when the day's work was finished he would sit by the kitchen fire in the French farm-houses, received by them as one of the family."

Facing page 24

" By that route came back the wounded . . . . Ever did the German artillery play on it, taking toll of all its traffic, of runners, ration-carriers, stretcher-bearers, wounded."

Facing page 40

" Its surroundings peopled by so many of Australia's dead, the site of the old wind-mill has since been sacred to Australian soldiers. But it was unlucky as a landmark and a thing of ill-omen in those days . . . . . "

Facing page 48

" . . . . . the passage of the river of mud which led to Mouquet Farm. And those at the tail end of the column waited for clearance . . . . waited in the gathering darkness when shells seem to fall so closely, and blunted sense of direction gives such false judgment of their location."

Facing page 54

" . . . trench feet . . . . their feet wrapped in cotton-wool, they limped along or negotiated a particularly difficult bit of ground on the shoulders of a passing digger. A weird sight presenting a sordid picture of war, weirder for the suggestion it obtruded on the onlooker of a schoolboy game in some happy play-ground."

Facing page 66

" Such was the Colonel, a man who lived with men and they despised him not'."

Facing page 84

" Seen against the dull glowering sky of the October evening, ruined Ypres looked a dreary place."

Facing page 96

". . . . . Captain Cumming . . . . An officer who loved a puzzling situation for its own sake."

Facing page 124

" In the shelter of one such ravine . . . . the men had a prolonged halt, and as the early morning had put appetites on edge all sat down to bully-beef and biscuits with much relish. Whilst so engaged, a low-flying enemy aeroplane swooped over and fired its machine-gun on them. . . . . ."

Facing page 138

" Down by the small spur known as Dean Copse some of them were laid to rest. . . . . . "

Facing page 152

MAPS.

The Department de la Somme	*Facing page*	28
The Battalion's Defence of the Amiens Road ..	,, ,,	120
The Battalion's Assault on Monument Wood ..	,, ,,	128
The Battalion's Position in the Hindenburg Line ..	,, ,,	148

A WORD TO THE SURVIVORS OF THE 48TH.

This record is written of the Battalion as a whole. I have not laid emphasis, though often warranted, on the part played by any individual, with one exception of which you would approve. Something of the spirit of the Battalion I have endeavoured to give. Something of its tragedy, perhaps too much for the conventional patriot. Something of its humour, perhaps too little. For I have not exploited the alleged humour of warfare. Humour might have scope in the back areas. In the humour of the trenches one could mostly see but the hysteria of tragedy.

Of the unit's many changes and incidents I have aimed at an accurate chronicle, to enable you live again in your own musings a past that no pen could recall. Whatever its value, I offer it in return for friendship unstinted from the morn of the Battalion in the East till the close of its day in the West.

W. DEVINE.

On the Meuse, 1919.

The Story of a Battalion.

Chapter I.

FORMATION OF THE BATTALION.

THIS tale of "arms and the man" opens on the 3rd of March, 1916. A party of officers and men of the 16th Battalion stood lined up on the parade-ground in the large Australian camp at Tel-el-Kebir. Altogether they numbered but four officers and three hundred and fifty of other ranks. The colonel of the 16th was addressing the assembled men. With blunt but sympathetic directness he was telling them that they were leaving the 16th Battalion, they were going on the strength of a new formation to be known as the 48th Battalion, they were all right good fellows whom he was very sorry to lose, but that the exigencies of the service demanded it, and he was quite certain they would give a good account of themselves in their new unit and prove worthy of their old Battalion.

The brief speech apparently so conventional was full of unwelcome significance to all present; to the intently listening soldiers it had the pathos of a farewell. No man is more susceptible to a bit of manly sentiment than the Australian soldier. The men liked their old colonel. Personal courage counts much with the soldier, and this colonel's courage had given his name to a bit of ground on Gallipoli. They liked their old Battalion, for the 16th had come through the campaign on Gallipoli, and that was at the time their criterion

B

of worth. Now they were being detailed to one of the "warbaby" formations, and even as the colonel spoke they eyed with some resentment a tall officer standing near to him. He was not unknown to many of them, for he too had been at Gallipoli. But to them he was an alien, of another Battalion, indeed of another Brigade, and the soldier is ever a regimental bigot. They were willing to admire him from a distance, but here he was presented as about to assume that close, domestic relationship involved in being one of them and the commander of them. That officer was Major R. L. Leane, appointed from the 11th Battalion to command the new formation. With a curt "Thank you" and salute to the Colonel, he now came forward, gave the order "48th Battalion 'shun," marched them off, and their inclusion in the 48th was an accomplished fact before their gloomy anticipation of it had ceased.

The men marched to another part of the camp where a working party had already erected two lines of tents. There they halted whilst the few officers busied themselves with details as to the allotting of tents. Captain Woollard, the medical officer of the new unit, was present, a strange figure in a pair of slacks with cap perched on the back of his head. He was critically eyeing the crowd, for he had seen many of their kind during his sojourn on Gallipoli, and was perhaps wondering how often he should deny the existence of their aches and ills. The quizzing diggers took careful stock of him also, wondering what manner of officer was this, as they filed into their tents with their various sections. They were to be much enlightened concerning him afterwards.

The week that followed saw other officers and non-commissioned officers join the new command, some reporting from other units, some coming from the Training Battalion. It was during this week that Captain A. P. Imlay reported for duty as second-in-command, and at the end of the week a draft of four officers and four hundred and six men came to the unit.

FORMATION OF THE BATTALION.

The more definite organisation of these details and of Battalion Headquarters now commenced. It was not an inspiring task, for the reinforcements were arriving very short of equipment, many of them without rifles and with little training. The greatest trouble, however, was the shortage of officers, and to remedy this a board was appointed in the Battalion to examine non-commissioned officers with a view to determining their suitability for commissions. A week later ten of these non-commissioned officers were promoted to the rank of Second-Lieutenant. On the 14th of the month Lieut. Ben. Leane reported from the Imperial Camel Corps and took on the duties of Adjutant to the Battalion.

The Battalion was now little short of full strength in men, and was daily receiving more officers. About this time, however, the unit was anything but a constant quantity. Parties of men would march into camp who, it would be afterwards discovered, were intended for other units, and to those units be finally forwarded after adding to the Battalion's numbers for a few days. It was a time too when reinforcements were plentiful, for Gallipoli had long ceased to take its toll of them, so Battalion commanders could afford to pick and choose. Consequently men were more readily transferred to other units than at a later date.

Although the Battalion was then showing daily fluctuations in its parade states, its personnel was typical of the class who continued to reinforce it throughout the period of its existence as a unit. West Australia sent its big, motley proportion, strong, hard men from the goldfields who had learned to give and take hard knocks in many a mining camp. Big loose-limbed fellows came from the back-blocks where timber-cutting and log-splitting provided their work and their play. Men came from the up-country stores, where the storeman has nothing in common with his anæmic colleague of the city, but is a brawny fellow accustomed to juggle with heavy sacks and between times with the burly form of a bushman inclined to be offensive in celebrating his visit to the township. There were blacksmiths and mining engineers, and men who worked on the railways, and men who would tell you with a laugh that they had never worked at all but had carried their swag from Fremantle to the Northern Territory.

From South Australia came farm-labourers hardened by that nomadic existence of the casual labourer. Came men of substance too, farmers and the sons of farmers, and completely lost their identity in the medley of khaki, a great leveller of social inequalities. If that identity was afterwards discovered, its discovery lay far apart from any reasons associated with their former position.

They were for the most part of the country, those men of the South and West, and therefore they were the best of material. Even those who came from the towns were not city-bred in the sense in which the term is generally understood. In that young land but few years had intervened between country and town. Their fathers had been of the fields. They themselves were accustomed to indulge a taste for the opener life of the country with a freedom not accorded to the city-born son of the old world. The life of the bush was in their blood, and so it was that the primitive conditions of active service found them easily adaptable to a life of campaigning.

And not a few there were who had come out to Australia from England, from Ireland, from Scotland, young fellows whose coming out in the first instance showed no lack of initiative, and whose endurance was further tested by the ups and downs of fortune that the immigrant encounters in Australia.

Of such was the 48th Battalion. They were not a kid-glove lot of men, and required something firmer than kid-glove handling. Those of them who drank, drank deep and were noisy in their cups and strong in their language. Most of them were at that time ill-trained soldiers, or not trained at all. Some of them were bad soldiers even after much

"They were, for the most part, of the country. . . . .
They were not a kid-glove lot of men. . . . ."

FORMATION OF THE BATTALION.

training. Very few of them proved bad fighters. All in all they were good fellows, with a manly simplicity of character that made them amenable as schoolboys to anyone in whom they had confidence or to whom they gave their friendship.

There was much delay about providing the Battalion with regular transport, and for several weeks there were but four horses on its strength. The colonel was mounted, as also were the second-in-command and the adjutant. The chaplain on being transferred from the Light Horse wisely brought his mount with him ; a fine horse, and how the chaplain came by him no one knew, whilst those who had a right to know indulgently refrained from pressing the question. Finally the company commanders were provided with hacks, and at the same time some draught horses and limbers arrived and formed the nucleus of a first-line transport. With them came a number of small-sized, vicious mules that proved utterly unmanageable and were happily left behind when the Battalion went away from Egypt.

Chapter II.

THE MARCH TO SERAPEUM.

TOWARDS the end of March the several Australian units camped at Tel-el-Kebir were under orders for employment on the defences of the Suez Canal. On the 27th of the month the 48th Battalion set out on its long journey of some forty-three miles across the desert. A camp at Serapeum was to be its resting place and training ground before occupying the front trenches.

There is nothing in a soldier's experience that involves more weary suffering than a march through the desert. The visitor to the seaside when crossing a sandy track keeps as near to the water's edge as possible, for there the receding tide has left the sand firm and compact. He is not unmindful of wet feet nor the effect of salt water on fine boots; but he prefers those risks to the painful plodding over that dry belt of sand further back where his feet sink with every step.

The soldier's circumstances are very different. When he changes his place of abode, and often does he change it when on active service, he must carry with him all the means and utilities of his daily life, the bed on which he sleeps, the utensils with which he eats his food, and that food itself—his rations for the day and the morrow. His pack contains a change of underwear, a second pair of boots, washing and shaving outfit, needles and cotton and buttons, besides all his little household gods in the shape of souvenirs and presents from home. His water-bottle is filled and adds not a little to the weight that is dragging at his neck, and his field-dressing flaps at his side pocket. When his personal necessities are thus attended to, the army makes its own use of him, giving him a rifle and bayonet to carry, and a trenching-tool and one hundred and twenty rounds of ammunition. That was "full marching order" on the way to Serapeum.

The Battalion started in the evening when the heat was less intense, and after marching twelve miles rested for the night. There were no tents nor shelter of any kind, and as often happens on the desert a cold night followed a very hot day. But the men were tired, and wrapped in their blankets they were soon asleep.

The late start had been a prudent thing as it allowed the march to be done in the comparative cool of the evening. It was resolved that on the next day advantage should also be taken of the early hours of the morning, before the sun became so intolerable. On the following morning, therefore, the journey was resumed about 8 o'clock. They marched only a distance of three miles, when a halt was made and all rested during the intense heat of the day. In the evening they again set out, and after marching for eight miles bivouaced.

It must be remembered that those men were not trained to march. There was no time for such training at Tel-el-Kebir, where the men were only gradually coming into camp, and where the heavy sands gave little scope for regular route-marching. Many of them came from Gallipoli, in whose trenches they had been cooped up for months. Many came from the dysentery wards of Cairo and Alexandria, a backwash of Gallipoli.

Now on this second day of their journey the hard conditions began to tell on them. Their boots were not fine, but of strong, formidable stuff, made to stand the test of rough roads and rough weather. In this fine, deep sand those boots became as dry and hard as well-seasoned timber.

The son of the desert wears sandals, for he would have as much as possible of the foot exposed to the air. He would have as little as possible of it so encased as to produce heat and moisture and consequent chafing. But those men came to the desert as clumsy novices, with high-topped service boots met by the closely-rolled puttee and with close-fitting breeches. And the desert had no pity on them. Wherever the minutest inlet showed itself in their coarse boots, the desert's sand entered to blister and chafe and raise red, tender blotches on their hot feet. The sun blazed mercilessly down upon them, menacing them with sun-stroke if they dared to discard their helmets, and matting their hair and making their eyes smart with trickling perspiration because they could not do so. The wind playing over the surface of the desert like the fitful ripple on a mountain lake, would now and then whirl the dust into their faces, there to form a sickly paste with the perspiration that bathed their brows and filled their ears and made a greasy dam on their bared chests. The desert refused them water, and when they had forced some from its few and reluctant pools and doctored it with their ill-smelling chemicals to guard themselves against the worse evils that lurked in it, the desert's scorching heat penetrated their cloth-bound water-bottles and made the water a tepid unwholesome thing that brought not refreshment and strength but nausea and weakness.

On they trudged, accomplishing so little, yet doing so much, marching in close formation with each file on the heels of the preceding one. The heavy smell of human sweat permeated the whole column, moving with the column, ever present with it because constantly generated by it, until it felt like being in a large, overcrowded, hot, reeking chamber that was slowly moving ahead. They were tired and weary men when at night they threw themselves on the sand to have a well-earned sleep.

Next morning the camp was astir very early, as the Battalion was to move off at 6 o'clock. Before some nine hundred men can be ready to start many things have to be done, and a Battalion commander takes no risks of being behind the time appointed. In those days the Battalion had no regular transport, and indeed heavy-wheeled limbers and

"..... those men came to the desert as clumsy novices, ... And the desert had no pity on them."

thirsty mules would have been of little avail on that trek with its deep sand and scanty water-supply. But a number of camels were allotted to the Battalion, and these led by their Indian guides stalked solemnly after the column. They were laden and over-laden, with such gear as could not be conveniently carried, stores, dixies and huge coppers for cooking the meals, officers' surplus gear that the loaders often insisted with lurid language could be very well done without, rations and some reserve supply of water. All these things had to be unloaded at each stage of the journey, and again loaded and ready for the march.

The hard conditions of the journey were not without their relieving features. No large gathering of Australian soldiers can ever be bereft of humour, and the more difficult their circumstances the more irrepressible is that humour. So when an officer who was unable to continue the march clumsily mounted a camel and immediately got pitched over its ears, the crowd roared with a lusty merriment that made it difficult to believe they presented such a sorry spectacle on the preceding evening. Things had been very busy on the third morning of the journey. But at last breakfast was over and the men had fallen in for the usual inspection. The sick parade had been held and the medical officer had handed out the last piece of sticking plaster for a sore heel, and told the patient he " just had to march whether he could or not." The rations were loaded and the quartermaster stood eyeing in uncertain manner a stove and copper that rested on the ground beside a camel. Then the Battalion commander walked up the lines and immediately the quartermaster endeavoured to look as alert and busy as possible. For the Battalion commander was in a vile mood ; things were not going too well ; his men were suffering, they were certain to be even worse off to-day, and he could do nothing more to help them. His eyes fell on the stove and copper not yet loaded on the camel, and the quartermaster got a bad time. The latter's several attempts at explanations were cut short with such insistent demands that they be got ready for transport immediately, that in desperation he forthwith had the stove and copper placed on the kneeling camel. Immediately there was a smell of singeing hair, a bellowing snort, and the camel dashed for the sky-line like a mad thing. The articles in question were quite hot after their use in cooking the morning meal, and the quartermaster had been patiently waiting for them to cool before placing them on the camel's back. They had plenty of time to cool afterwards, for they were of no further use to the Battalion after the camel had finished with them. But the immediate task of rescuing them gave the quartermaster an opportunity to get away from the commander and explanations.

Moasca was to be their next stage in the journey. This was the third day of the march, heavy packs felt heavier, the sun seemed to blaze worse than ever, and of water they had none.

The soldier on the march in a hot climate requires to be very sparing in his use of water. The old soldier drinks very little of it, and when the water becomes warm he does not drink it at all. He takes a mouthful, rinses his mouth, and then squirts it out again. Most of the time he jogs along with a small pebble in his mouth. But on the desert track to Serapeum there were few old soldiers. Most of them were very new soldiers and very young soldiers, and regardless of instructions they would often have exhausted their water-bottles long before the completion of the day's journey. A brilliant idea had occurred to someone by which this could be obviated, and a supply of water made available for the men at that stage of the day's march where they should most need it. During the midday halt on the preceding day all water-bottles were collected, stowed on camels, and some men detailed to go on ahead and meet the column on the following day with refilled bottles. This seemed alright and it enabled those who had been sparing of their water-bottles to have one glorious drink before parting with them.

THE MARCH TO SERAPEUM.

But many brilliant ideas fail in execution, and the practical working out of this one had several disadvantages. For camels are occasionally obstreperous animals, and on this occasion their Indian guides were found to be equally unsatisfactory. During the next day's march the men looked anxiously for the coming of those camels, but it was not until they were within two miles of Moasca that they appeared.

The water proved to be warm, sickly stuff, but it was not so regarded by those who drank it eagerly and greedily. The result was inevitable, and soon showed itself. Men fell out of the line of march and throwing themselves on the ground in a state of reckless exhaustion, rolled over to vomit in the sands. One hundred and twenty-four men thus fell out whilst the column continued on its way to Moasca.

Those who were left behind could be trusted to rejoin their unit, for ways and means never failed the Australian soldier whatever the army might sometimes think of his casual choice of them. They did not fail him on this occasion. When those soldiers had rested they struck across the desert to where they could see a black line trailing through the sands. It was the railway from Cairo, and when they had reached its hard, firm track they felt that buoyancy which only those who have trudged through the sands of Egypt can understand. In this way ninety-eight of them regained their unit; whilst others further improved the occasion by boarding a passing train which brought them to Serapeum, a day's journey ahead of the column.

The Battalion rested for the remainder of the day at Moasca. It was a good spell and afforded an opportunity of attending thoroughly to the many sore feet of all ranks. The next day's march lay along the banks of a fresh-water canal, and forty-three men unable to march were sent on to Serapeum by barge. The distance to camp was then about thirteen miles, and none fell out although the last few miles of the journey were done in the face of a blinding sand-storm.

CHAPTER III.

TRAINING FOR FRANCE.

The Battalion was now camped near to the banks of the Suez Canal, and the men spent much of their time swimming in its waters. Swimming parades were frequent and training began for aquatic sports to be held later on. This, combined with the daily routine of military work, soon turned those men into a Battalion of healthy, vigorous athletes. Moreover they were happy in mind, for expectation ran high of going to France at an early date. All were very tired of Egypt and looked to France as a happy release. Nevertheless it was not to France but some five miles further into the desert that they went on the 9th of April. There they settled down to vigorous training, rifle exercises, infantry attack in artillery formation, and outpost duty. Every day the monotonous routine of training went on, and every day Egypt's sun grew hotter. Whatever could be done to lessen the discomfort of that awful heat was done. Mess-sheds were erected to which the men could escape from the muggy, overpowering atmosphere of the bell-tents. Several times the business of training was combined with pleasure, a route-march being arranged to the banks of the canal. Those occasions were enjoyed as the happiest of holidays, officers and men immediately stripping for a swim, and afterwards going to their midday meal which on such days would be cooked at the canal and eaten in picnic fashion on the sands.

It was during one of these trips to the canal that some band instruments arrived at Serapeum, consigned to the

TRAINING FOR FRANCE.

Battalion. They consisted of a bass-drum, a kettle-drum and some fifes, and it was immediately resolved that the Battalion should be played back to camp by its regimental band. Company commanders called for any musicians that might be in their different companies. Volunteers for the big-drum were plentiful as also for the kettle-drum. Performers on the fife seemed to be fewer or more diffident, but eventually some were found and, to give the band a fuller appearance, a few others were impressed into the service. These latter were very reluctant and made remarks strongly reflecting on the family respectability of those comrades who had proclaimed them as promising musicians, remarks which seemed only to intensify the unselfish happiness of the aforesaid comrades at the recognition being given their friends' musical talent. Eventually the Battalion fell in to return to camp, and the fife-and-drum band proceeded to the head of the column and played its first march with very little fife and a great deal of drum.

On the banks of the Suez the Battalion celebrated its first Anzac Day on the 25th of April, when swimming sports were held. The Anzacs of the unit wore some red ribbon for the day to mark them out as veterans from their new comrades-in-war, who were so unfortunate or so fortunate as not to have participated in that adventure. There were a good many of those Anzacs present, men who little knew what great adventures the war still had in store for them.

On the 5th of May the Battalion marched from the railhead, where they were then encamped, to Habieta. The Turks were expected to attempt another attack on the Suez Canal, and a line of outposts strongly wired had already been constructed, stretching north and south far along the desert. Habieta was some twelve miles from the canal on its eastern side, and here the Battalion took up its position in the trenches.

Whatever the higher military authorities may have known, and let us concede to them a mysterious prescience, the amateur mind looking back upon that system of defences is puzzled to explain its utility. The passage of an army across that harsh desert from the direction feared, and the conservation by it of a striking-force capable of overcoming the weakest defence, looked like an attempt of the impossible. Yet it was on the presumption of such an impossibility that this particular line of defence seemed based.

Measures had to be taken however even to guard against the impossible, and it was not a weak defence that awaited the anticipated attack. There was plenty of hard work, for in the constantly shifting sand the trenches had to be revetted with sandbags. Every sandstorm that blew across the desert, filled up the trenches again until one could scarcely trace the outline of them in its shining surface; and then the monotonous work of clearing them recommenced. Old wire entanglements long constructed had been covered and recovered and rendered useless for their purpose by the surging sand. These had to be made formidable once more and further reinforced.

But whatever its utility for its immediate purpose, the period in the trenches at Habieta was good training for the days of more serious war that lay ahead. All anticipated an attack, indeed longed for an attack. There was therefore brought to the different duties a keenness of spirit that cannot be attained in the routine of camp training. Approaching an outpost in the darkness one heard the businesslike snap of the lock of a rifle and the barked out challenge showed the sentries' tense alertness. "Stand to arms" for an hour before dawn in that country where dawn came so early, involved a rigid inclusion of all ranks, even of those who had no arms to "stand to" as the Colonel readily informed the medical officer and the chaplain.

On the whole the days were enjoyed by everybody. The men had hard work but advantage was taken of the cooler conditions in the early morning and in the evening, and during the intense heat of the day they rested. Besides daily life now began to hold something more like the "real thing" than the training of the camp with its incessant drill, its manœuvres and sham attacks. The Australian soldier is always more satisfied to use his spade in the trenches whether they be of sand or of mud. He is more satisfied to crawl over the parapet before dawn and sit throughout the long, lonely day in a sniper's post, relying for his security on the bunch of grass that camouflages his helmet. He will proclaim in expressive language that he vastly prefers these things to "sloping arms and forming fours like a blanky automaton."

The Turk was awaited in vain, however, and as his coming became more and more improbable there were no regrets when the Battalion moved back to camp at the railhead, which it did on the 19th of May.

Here preparations for France began in real earnest. The Battalion was now considerably over strength, and arrangements were immediately made to send the surplus men to the training camp at Tel-el-Kebir. Quite a large number left the unit in this manner and were inconsolable at their fate. But they soon afterwards rejoined in France, where the Battalion's first engagement was to leave many vacant places. All articles of equipment short of establishment were supplied, and the sun-helmets and light, khaki tunics laid aside for Australian hats and service dress that should be necessary in the cooler climate to which they were now going.

At this time the generality of the 48th men, whilst regarding their Battalion as a constituent unit of the 12th Brigade, would only in a hazy manner recognise it as a part of the 4th Division. Afterwards they developed a very definite recognition of the fact, and learned to discuss with stimulated eloquence the rights and wrongs of the 4th Division in many an estaminet throughout northern France. It is interesting to note that during those days of final preparation for embarkation it acted for the first time as a complete Division, practising a night operation in which the 48th Battalion took part. It was a bit of mimic warfare, the precursor of many operations in real warfare which the Division was afterwards to perform.

It was a Battalion complete in every detail and over one thousand in strength that marched from the railhead on the 27th of May to await entraining at Serapeum. On the night of the 1st of June it entrained, and arrived at Alexandria next morning, where it immediately embarked for France. The conveying troopship was the "Caledonia," with Captain Black as skipper, and she sailed two days later. Both ship and master later on earned some notability—the ship when she was torpedoed and sunk during a subsequent voyage on the same seas; and to a greater degree Captain Black when he was captured and taken on board a German submarine under circumstances that cost Captain Fryatt his life. Only England's threat of the sternest reprisals prevented the same fate being meted out to Black.

Life on board was the ordinary routine of troopship life, its most pleasant feature being its brief duration. The submarine guard told the usual lies as to the number of submarines they had seen. The usual board was appointed to examine the complaints concerning the men's food and compel the chief steward to supply more meat and fewer rotten potatoes.

A startling break in the monotony was caused by the receipt of a wireless to the effect that Lord Kitchener had been lost in the "Hampshire." Australians had seen very little of Kitchener, but they had heard much of his stern ways and of his uncompromising manner of dealing with that class of officer who can so order his life as to see very little soldiering, and who is loved not by the men of the rank and file. And there were old soldiers of the South African campaign among them, who told tales of surprise visits by Kitchener to various bases, when he is alleged to have expressed the crisp alternative "to the front by the first train or to England by the first boat." Perhaps Kitchener had shared those preconceptions of the Australian soldier, so monotonously entertained by many English military men. It is idle to speculate now, yet one is inclined to think that the Australian soldier would have liked Kitchener, and that Kitchener might have got to like the Australian soldier. Anyhow among those men on the "Caledonia" there was much honest regret for his untimely fate.

At last the ship pulled into Marseilles, and the Battalion disembarking on the 9th of June entrained immediately for the north of France. The train journey lasted from 5 o'clock on Friday evening till Monday morning. The men travelled in cattle trucks. Thirty men were assigned to each truck, and every man had with him his bulky pack and equipment. But the travellers forgot their discomforts as they drank in the beauties of the scenery. Lovely France! Yes, thrice lovely after the verdureless glare of the Egyptian desert. A passing troop-train never fails to attract people out-of-doors, the women from their housework, the men from the stables and the cowsheds, and in those days the Australian's slouch hat was a less common thing in France than at a later period. So as the train slowly meandered through the villages, old men—for there seemed to be no young men in the country —and women hurried out to greet the passing Australians. Children burst riotously from their homes to run along the train and cry shrilly for souvenirs.

They were such scenes as made pathetic appeal to those soldiers. Here were not the coloured people of crafty, complex Egypt, but men and women who recalled the people of their own distant home-land. They would have made friends of the little children of Egypt also, for the children of all lands are above the distinctions of race or even of colour. But the children of the East, with their fly-worried eyes and lips, required a woman's care before they could gain a man's affection. It was different with these clean-limbed, healthy tomboys who ran by the train crying for souvenirs, and to

C

whom the soldiers threw their few remaining Egyptian coins, the badges of their hats, the buttons of their tunics and their army biscuits.

The train arrived in the north of France on the morning of the 12th and the Battalion detrained at Bailleul. The weather had now become raw and cold, and heavy rain was falling as the unit marched to Merris, a village some few miles distant.

CHAPTER IV.

IN FRANCE.

IN the farm-houses around Merris the Battalion had its first experience of billets. To this experience all looked forward. Imposed regularity is never congenial, and the lines of tents of the fixed camp entail much regularity and supervision. This is not so easily maintained when men are billeted among a civilian population scattered over a wide area. But their introduction to billets was under the most unfavourable conditions. The barns and outhouses in which the men slept were often very draughty, whilst for the remainder of the month of June the weather was cold and rain fell almost constantly. It was in marked contrast with the climate which they had left at the beginning of the month, and many were soon suffering from colds.

Nevertheless all ranks settled down to happy enjoyment of their new manner of lodgment. It was found to be disappointing in so far as it had promised any greater freedom from military restraint and duties, for parades came as regularly as formerly and had to be as punctiliously attended. Life in billets had other compensations however, and in whatever farmhouse the soldiers found themselves they soon had "the run of the place."

The Australian soldier is an adaptable being, wisely tolerant of a strange civilisation, and ever ready to get into sympathy with a strange people. At night when the day's work was finished he would sit by the kitchen-fire in the French farm-houses, received by them as one of the family. When the old grandfather would pour into his ear a long yarn of the campaign of " Soixante-dix," the Australian would listen sympathetically and murmur " Oui, Oui," though he understood not half of what was being said. When the old woman went to the well for water, the Australian would be there to turn the handle of the quaint pulley, to unhook the bucket off the chain and carry it back to the house. Of an evening he might be seen going off with the daughters of the house to milk the cows, and returning with two pails of milk swinging from a pole on his neck and shoulders after the fashion of the French peasantry.

It was this easy good-nature and innate, unaffected courtesy which gained for him the place he has since occupied in the affections of the French people. For the most part the only people left in the houses were old men, women-folk and children, and in his brief sojourn in the different villages, the Australian casually took the place of the grown-up son of the family and as such was recognised with uproarious merriment. The Madame made him innumerable cups of coffee. The girls sewed the colour patches and the buttons on his tunic, and performed the many other odd jobs of needlework that fall to the soldier on active service. The little fellows of the house played with him, called him " Deegair," and climbed on his knee to snatch the wide-brimmed hat off his head, that hat which was a continual source of interest and of envy to the French boy. The baby had no fear of him, but would crow with delight when he perched it on his shoulder and carried it down the village street, calmly ignoring the good-humoured badinage which his grinning comrades shouted at him from every corner.

In some parts the small tradespeople robbed him, doing so in perfectly legal fashion, but none the less effectively. They had the tendency of their class to make hay whilst the sun shone, and the digger had plenty of money and all the soldier's readiness to spend it. So price-lists that were reasonable to civilian customers made very exorbitant demands of the soldier.

Sometimes the small farmers were equally zealous in their efforts to rob his regiment, again in quite a legal manner. No enactment regarding the billeting of foreign troops is better known to the civilian population of northern France and Belgium, than that which authorises them to make a *reclamation* on the regiment for any damage or loss occasioned by its soldiers. It is an attractive method of making money, since in the subsequent enquiry it is held sufficient if the damage is proved to have been done by soldiers of that regiment. The matter is seldom brought home to the individual soldiers involved, so it is the regiment that pays, and damages are always held to be more easily borne by a corporation than by an individual. When the soldier helped himself to a few of Madame's chickens it was generally known what particular section of the unit had benefited, for chickens create a great row when being caught and a great smell when being cooked. The culprit would readily admit the offence, the men of his section who had partaken of the feast would cheerfully subscribe the amount demanded by Madame, usually twice the value of the chickens, and a sensible platoon officer would hand over the money and say nothing more about the matter. It was different, however, when at the end of a three weeks' sojourn in a village, claims began to amass at the Battalion Headquarters for damage done to crops by soldiers taking short cuts across the fields, for trees cut down by the Battalion cooks to reinforce the scanty supply of firewood allowed them, for clean straw which the soldiers carried from Madame's stacks to make themselves more comfortable beds. These claims could not be brought home to individual soldiers, and fortunately so, for otherwise the soldiers would seldom have drawn pay. The claims were always excessive, the claimant was usually a Madame with all a woman's faculty of exaggeration and of indignant remonstrance. So the regiment paid, sometimes the full amount claimed, and perhaps always more than enough.

Yet they were a fine people, those French peasants. And those French women who so bravely managed the farms during the absence of their menfolk at the war, who during four years of that war had to do a man's work in the fields and a man's work in the markets—who can blame them if they were determined to lose nothing by the soldiers and even gain a little from the soldiers ? Tradespeople, even tradespeople living in peaceful remoteness from the theatre of war, who sell anything to Jack of the navy, to Tommy or to the Digger, never lose anything by the transaction. His uniform belies his stinted means, his air and manner suggest prodigality, and the sleek man of business regards him as legitimate game. Billeting a foreign army that had come far to help them had long ago lost its glamour of sentiment for those French peasants, and was now rated at its market value. They were a sorely tried people who had to carry on the daily work of their farms, whilst their homes were overrun by soldiers constantly coming and going. The Australian indeed seemed to show a ready understanding of their difficulties. Himself generally a man of the fields he was careful of their crops, and gave little cause for *reclamations*. He did sometimes cut down their trees, for coming from his own bush-land, where wood is all too plentiful, he could not readily appreciate the present parsimony. But he often changed Madame's sorrow into joy by chopping an equal amount of firewood for her, and presenting it with much grinning politeness and bad French. In his leisure hours he would lend a hand at gathering the crops, and Madame could always be certain of his prompt help in the odd jobs around a farm-house that call for a man's strength.

In this way did the Australian soldier become a most popular figure throughout northern France. However late at night his Battalion marched away from any village, the whole population remained out of bed to bid him farewell. The French were no less popular with the Australian. In his far-off land he had none of those insular prejudices against "the continental" which the war has done much to remove from the people of the British Isles. He came prepared to like the French people as he is prepared to like any people worth liking. He found the French worth liking and he liked them.

The Battalion settled down to these conditions during the month of June. Training was resumed immediately. Officers and men went off to different schools of instruction in bayonet-fighting, in bombing, in sniping. Here shrapnel helmets were issued for the first time, and the men got their first instruction in the precautions to be taken against gas. The box-respirator of later days was then unknown and they received the old form of gas-mask, in which they practised marching, advancing to attack and various movements.

These things were all characteristic of the war on the Western front, to them a new and unfamiliar war, and everyone yearned to see it at closer quarters. Of a morning the guns could be heard in the distance, but in that quiet country district removed from the main lines of military traffic, there was no other indication of war.

The next destination of the Battalion and the task to be allotted to it was always a favourite topic of conversation, and during those few weeks many rumours were abroad. Finally on the 3rd of July the Battalion marched towards the sound of the guns, until it arrived at the village of Doulieu, where it was billeted for the night. Next day the march was resumed, the river Lys was crossed at Sailly. That night the men had their first experience of German shrapnel, bursting high and ineffectively over their heads as they entered the village of Fleurbaix.

Two of the companies immediately went on to the support line of trenches, whilst the remaining companies were billeted in the village. The village was occasionally shelled heavily, the church and several other buildings had been badly damaged. But quite a number of civilians still remained in the place, retiring to great cellars under their houses whilst danger lasted. During the day it was usually so peaceful that one could scarcely believe the German trenches were but a short distance away.

In the support trenches things were almost equally quiet. The ground was low and marshy and there was much draining of communication-saps, cleaning out of old trench shelters and laying down of fresh duckboards. Very few shells fell in the area, and only some minor casualties were sustained by the Battalion during its term there.

Even a visit to comrades in other Battalions in the front line did not afford much greater interest. The weather was now warm, and men who had been out on patrol the previous night might be seen hanging around listlessly, playing cards with a weary, disinterested air, or stretched out on the duckboards asleep. Others manned the look-out post and occasionally fired a shot across no-man's-land at "Parapet-Joe," an elusive German sniper who was almost the sole source of interest during the day. At night or in the early morning things were sometimes lively enough. Taken generally the front line at Fleurbaix was a disappointment, and all ranks considered that either the war in France was much over-rated or they had not seen the war in France. That they had not yet seen the war in France proved afterwards to be the true explanation.

On the night of the 12th the Battalion was relieved by troops of the Fifth Australian Division, which suffered so heavily a week later in its attack launched from the same trenches. That same night the unit marched back to Doulieu, and next day set out again for Merris which was reached about 8 o'clock in the evening.

The second stay at Merris was but a short one, for the Fourth Australian Division was then under orders to proceed to the Somme. So on the morning of the 14th the Battalion entrained at Bailleul and arrived at Doullens in the evening. The detraining of the transport, of horses and mules, of

"The Australian soldier is an adaptable being, ... At night when the day's work was finished he would sit by the kitchen fire in the French farm-houses, received by them as one of the family."

limbers and cookers was a tedious business, and a considerable time had elapsed before the Battalion started for Berteaucourt.

The march was a long one, about fifteen miles. The men had had an early breakfast, and since then had been travelling in an overcrowded troop-train where it was impossible to give them their regular mid-day meal. No hot meal was ready for them when they detrained, for standing orders regarding troop-trains strictly forbade the lighting of fires in cookers during the train journey. The Battalion was then comparatively new to standing orders regarding troop-trains and conscientiously obeyed them. Moreover the late arrival of the train had made further delay impossible if Berteaucourt was to be reached that night. So the men started off on their long march with light stomachs, and with heavy packs that had become a little heavier by the addition of the steel helmet and gas-mask which were now part of their equipment.

It is not a very uncommon thing for a soldier to fall out on the line of march, and certainly it is not a sight which his comrades view sadly. Yet if he be not a known malingerer he is deserving of all sympathy. Perhaps he has been at the head of the column, and as file after file goes past he is lying at the side of the road, reclining on the pack which he has been too weary to remove from his shoulders ; his hat pushed back from his brow, his rifle fallen across his outstretched legs, his hand loosely grasping his uncorked water bottle, his eyes looking surly defiance at his grinning comrades. He has "given in" and though he and they fully agree that soldiers should not have to carry such heavy burdens, that soldiers should not have to march at all, still it is "giving in," and " giving in" is generally thought to deserve at the best to be treated with a good-humoured contempt. His platoon officer has already stopped with him for one strenuous moment, to tell him he has brought disgrace irreparable on the fair name of the platoon. Then the poor fellow runs the gauntlet of the passing column's humour, mock concern for his health, advice on his choice of a more suitable career, and apparently harmless references to the motion of swinging lead which never fail to draw the most violent language from him who has fallen by the wayside. When finally he is interviewed by the medical officer at the rear of the column, he is usually in a state of defiance and ill-temper that enable him to do but scant justice to himself in stating his probably good reasons for falling out of the march.

Men thus fell out on the march to Berteaucourt. Darkness came and the pace of the Battalion slackened and became uneven on the hilly road, and the column proceeded with that concertina movement so hateful to the exponents of good marching. Berteaucourt was finally reached at midnight.

CHAPTER V.
LA SOMME.

At Berteaucourt the Battalion was now for the first time in the *department de la Somme*, that part of France in which it was to spend most of its period of work and of relaxation, of fighting and of resting, during the whole future course of the war. The river from which the *department* takes its name enters it where Ham is situated at its south-eastern corner, flows north through Peronne, then zig-zags westward through the centre of the *department* passing near Bray and near Corbie on its way to Amiens, again slightly northward on to Abbéville and to the sea. Here it is river, there it is canal, but ever its waters flow peacefully, whilst the flourishing towns and pretty villages it once skirted have perished to make it famous.

It was in this *department* that the Battalion had its first encounter in the war of the Western Front, at Pozières which lay just within its borders. Afterwards the unit left for the trenches of Flanders, but returned to it to lie for several weeks at Flers and Gueudecourt looking over at Bapaume. Then Bapaume enticed the men of the 48th outside its limits, where they were badly used at Bullecourt and once more hurried back to their old *department* to count their dead and fill their vacant places.

Yet again they left it, this time for a long spell in the North, and got on very well in a series of engagements beginning with Messines. They remained away until they fared very badly at Passchendaele, and immediately they struck misfortune set out once more for their familiar territory, and marched to its extreme corner where the *department* meets the sea.

In the beginning of 1918 they returned to the North and for a time enjoyed themselves immensely, until they had to rush away from their sports and games, their cinematograph shows and concerts to help defend its capital. Finally a few weeks before the armistice was signed, they crossed its eastern boundaries for their last engagement with the enemy, and some nights later stole away from the new ground which they had won from him, and marching till dawn were again within its limits.

Amiens is in the heart of the *department* and is the mainspring of all its activities. After the first great enemy onslaught of 1914 the battle-line had settled on its eastern half, cutting it north and south and lying dangerously near to its centre. Some distance behind the German trenches lay French towns and villages. So fast was the rush of the first advance that their capture had involved but slight damage, and the inhabitants settled down to such normal activities of life as the conditions of German occupation allowed them.

Then in the middle of 1916 the enemy's tide-line of fortification and defence, which seemed to have become stable for all time, began to recede under strong and constant pressure. Not regularly and evenly did it recede, but over each district it moodily ebbed and flowed, its fringe and its back-wash devouring the towns and villages, the farms and orchards, that it had spared in its first sweeping advance. Slowly and fitfully it went back, leaving all its war's residue of filth to mark its ebb, crumpling up railroads, disfiguring the broad, clean highways, wiping out the peaceful country lanes, strewing with wreck the fertile lands and smiling plains, and carrying with it what remained of the panic-stricken inhabitants.

Only at the eastern borders of the *department* did the devastating wave rest. There the armies that followed its

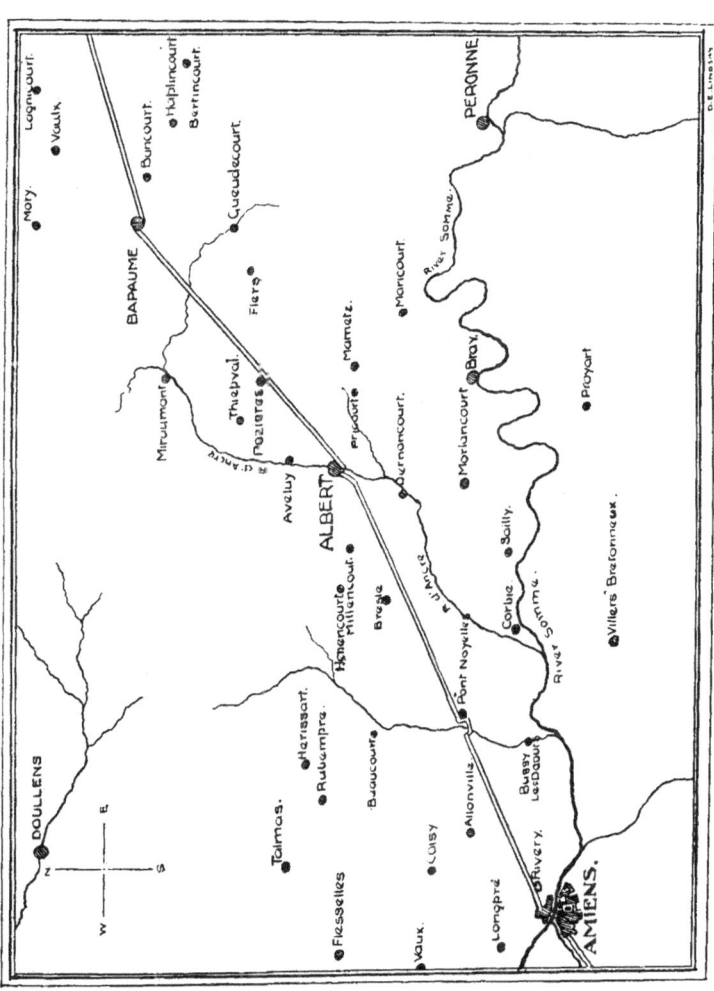

Map showing the Department de la Somme (drawn to scale).

Facing p. 28.

receding water-line were blocked by a barrier which seemed to make intrusion impossible. Behind that barrier its waters piled up again, gradually swelling all through the summer of 1917 and through the following winter. Then in the spring, like those floods that come with the melting of the winter's snows, they again burst forth, and again they swept over the land from which they had so reluctantly receded. This time the menacing wave had far to go before there was any civilian life to disorganise, any quiet farms and happy villages ; but it had in abundance the whole intricate organisation and works of a great military life, and on them it fed to satiety its appetite for destruction. Men and horses and guns, hospitals and workshops and railroads all were engulfed by it. Many were caught by it even as they fled from it as from something preternatural. Others stood against it only to be tossed on its crest, as it surged on towards its old line. Even that did not prove to be its high tide, for it swept still further on, making for the heart of the *department* it had already so foully used.

The heart, Amiens, it did not reach. A breakwater intervened against which it spent its strength ; and with a suddenness almost as dramatic as its westward flow, it again receded towards the East until it had left the hills and valleys of the Somme far behind.

Just as the river runs through the *department* from East to West so does a broad main highway from its south-western to its north-eastern corner bisect it diagonally. This is the Amiens-Bapaume road which crosses the river at Amiens. Along this road are several places of poignant interest to a member of the 48th Battalion. When he has left Amiens behind and is approaching the outskirts of Albert, he comes to that part of the road where it is crossed by the old railway line, and where his Battalion formed one of those obstacles that blocked the western passage of the great tide in its second rush towards Amiens. When he has passed through Albert and continued but a short distance on the same road, he may even now see an unshapely mound on his left. It is all that remains of the old wind-mill that marked the highest point on the Pozières Ridge. Near the wind-mill lie many of the 48th's dead. There the Battalion had its first engagement on the Western Front when in two days' fighting five-hundred and ninety-eight officers and men were thinned from its ranks, what time the battle-line so reluctantly receded eastwards after its first long menace of the West. When he goes further along and approaches the outskirts of the *department* he may see on his right what remains of Flers and Gueudecourt, where the Battalion spent most of the severe winter of 1916-17 and there fought against all the rigours and dull misery of trench-life. If he leaves Bapaume and follows the road as it veers round to the east on its way to Cambrai, he may look over to that country around Noreuil on his left and leading towards Bullecourt, where his Battalion offered its second great holocaust in the spring of 1917.

Such great happenings had their being in the *department de la Somme*, and such mighty interests had it in store for the men of the 48th Battalion who were now for the first time billeted within its boundaries. But in those first days at Berteaucourt no one thought of the future, the present offered sufficient food for reflection ; for the Battalion in its march from Doullens to Berteaucourt had " made a bad march."

When many men fall out on the line of march, and time is wasted and the general military appearance of the unit suffers, there is always a violent commotion afterwards. What the Battalion commander has to say to his senior officers is religiously handed on by them to their immediate juniors, until it reaches the sergeants of the different sections who impose it with lurid additions on men of noted inclination to fall by the wayside. In this case there was more than one Battalion and apparently more than one Brigade involved. The proverbial luck in numbers availed not, however, to afford escape from the Battalion commander, from the Brigadier, and finally from the Divisional commander who swore that his Brigades should be taught to march.

The Divisional commander at that time was Major-General Sir H. V. Cox. He was not exactly a genial man, that old Indian soldier, with a little of the heat of India's sun in his temper. He is remembered best in his casual encounters with the digger on the roads or about the camp, when he would put the embarrassed Australian through a strict cross-examination, firing questions at him with quick, jerky utterance and a most unfriendly air. One is inclined to think that he may have arranged those situations and affected much of that manner for his own enjoyment of the digger. Certain it is that he lacked not appreciation of the Australian soldier, nor lacked the will to give emphatic expression to it long after he left the Division. That his caustic words were not unrelieved by humour could have been seen on Christmas Day of the same year, when he strolled round the billets of the 48th Battalion and the diggers greeted him with scant ceremony but with a cheery grin and " a merry Christmas, Mister Cox." It was a well tried Division before he left it, and many of those who lived under his strict régime still credit his foundation of it with much of its subsequent success.

General Cox was not in an amiable mood, however, towards the several Battalions that had just arrived in the Somme area, and immediately the most vigorous training was begun. Reveille was at 6 a.m. From 6.30 a.m. till 7.30 a.m. there was drill. After breakfast followed a route-march over a distance of nine or ten miles in full marching order. From 2 p.m. until 5.30 p.m. training went on again, and at night there was instruction in Lewis Gun work from 7 p.m. till 9 p.m., at which all officers were bound to attend. The programme of training and instruction went on daily, and daily the heavy route-marching was gone through; until every road and hedge-row and farm-house in the surrounding district had become monotonously familiar, and the men asked one another with humorous sarcasm what work had brought them to France, "whether they had come to fight or to go touring the country like blanky Cook's Tourists."

The days at Berteaucourt were withal very happy ones. The hours of relaxation were enjoyed the more for the hard work which preceded them. In no part of France did the men make more friends among the civilian population. It was the first time that the Battalion had been billeted in a normal French village, with convenient access to its many estaminets. In this village estaminets were numerous, and those were the days when champagne was plentiful. Perhaps that "champagne" was inferior to champagne, but it was not inferior to what afterwards fetched high prices under the same name. The soldier's pocket was quite equal to it. The soldier's many celebrations, occasioned by anything from a victory over a neighbouring Battalion in the football-field to a victory over Fritz in the battle-field, could in his estimation be properly honoured by no other drink. At these celebrations he drank, and sometimes drank deep.

Of those French estaminets it might be said that in general the entertainment provided by them was not much abused. Utterly unlike the drinking-bars of English-speaking countries whose patrons enter, drink and are then expected to make way for others, the estaminet approximated more to the English inn of Dickens and of the pre-Victorian era. The corner of shelves containing many-coloured bottles of wines and of syrupy liqueurs, represented but a small part of the activities of its roomy interior. In the centre of it there was usually a large stove, where Madame cooked many plates of chipped potatoes and many golden omelettes for the diggers, as they sat around the several tables admiring the operation. At the stove also Madame prepared the Australian's many cups of coffee, whilst Madame's daughter remained on duty at the shelves to dole out the rum which was to be added to it. Around those tables the soldiers were free to remain throughout the evening, discussing their great doings of the past, and greater imaginings. Madame used a woman's tact to prevent excess, because she had a woman's business shrewdness to guard against her estaminet being put out-of-bounds by the Battalion authorities if excess occurred. Punctually the picquet came to empty out at bed-time those who had imbibed too freely, using a friendly insistence and the help of the soldiers who had not imbibed at all.

The many who did not take strong drink were not left uncatered for by the all-providing estaminet. Their presence was always welcome to Madame for the restraining influence on the few who were liable to become difficult. Madame's coffee was perfect, even without the addition of rum, and this they could sip whilst they smoked and made of the estaminet their club.

The soldier on active service is necessarily an out-of-doors man. During the day he seldom goes to his billet except to put on his equipment for parade, or leave it there when parade is dismissed. He is quite content with his billet for its two purposes, storing his belongings and housing his bed when he adjourns to it after the fatigues of the day. But the hut or farm-shed allotted to some twenty soldiers, is usually a cheerless, draughty place by day, and a congested, dimly-lit place by night. So during the long nights the lights and cleanliness and warmth of the estaminet afforded a happy release to the soldier, when resting behind the lines. Afterwards organisation advanced in this as in all other details of military life and work, and every effort was made within the army itself to brighten the soldier's hours of relaxation. Of concert-halls and recreation-huts and entertainment-troupes that were then made available, he made full use. In a fighting unit, however, ever marching from place to place, such organisation was often disorganised. For such units the estaminet continued to serve, only to a lesser degree, the same useful purpose which it had served in the beginning.

In the back areas there were also other places where entertainment was of a much more harmful kind, and where the soldier was liable to that risk of demoralisation which can never be dissociated from the life of a great campaign. These lay far back, however, in the large towns at the base, with which the Battalion never came in contact. Speaking generally it might be said that the normal life of the fighting unit in France, represented something far more pure-minded and morally healthy than is maintained by a similar body of men in civil life.

Thus the days at Berteaucourt went on until the 27th of the month, when the Battalion marched away on the road to Toutencourt, a village lying towards the east where the great battle was even then raging. That was the first battle of the Somme, and the men of the 48th had as yet but the most indefinite rumours of it. They spent the night under canvas at Toutencourt and two days later were again in comfortable billets at Harponville, a small village in the neighbourhood.

On the 1st of August they left Harponville, and resuming the march eastwards soon saw Albert in the distance, and saw for the first time the leaning figure of the Virgin on its church spire. The Battalion did not enter the town, for every now and then shells landed in it throwing up clouds of dust and smoke and debris from its piled masonry, and troops went through its streets quickly and only in small parties at long intervals. So the unit rested on the western side of Albert and made preparations to bivouac near an old brick-fields there, whilst awaiting instructions as to what part it was expected to play in the battle of the Somme.

Chapter VI.

POZIERES RIDGE.

THE 48th Battalion had not as yet any experience of life in the immediate front line trenches on the western front. Whilst it lay near Fleurbaix in reserve or in the support trenches, duty had taken some members of the Battalion to the front line. Others were induced by curiosity to make stolen excursions. The sight did not impress nor interest them over much. The construction of the defence works was interesting. In that marshy country where the spade so readily struck water, a deep wall of sand-bags rising some eight feet above the ground had to take the place of the impracticable trench. Mounting the fire-step of its deep traverses, they could see over the parapet to where the enemy's wire entanglements began some eighty yards away. The dull grey wall stretched further north and away towards the south, and the enemy's defences maintained their parallel course with it.

The enemy contained himself within his strong line, secure in its power of defence and confident in its advantage as a jumping-off ground for further advance. That strong line entered the *department de la Somme* on the north of Beaumont Hamel. It then crossed to the left bank of the Ancre and enveloped in its course the high and advantageous ground around Thiepval, which stretched to Pozières some two miles eastward and there reached its greatest altitude. From Thiepval the enemy's line ran south. Passing through the western outskirts of Fricourt it made the village the apex of a formidable salient by running sharply eastward beyond Maricourt before it again veered towards the south. Up to this point the British trenches ran parallel with it from the north. Here, a short distance north of the Somme, the British garrison linked up with the French. By the latter the Allies' long line of defence was carried across the river and followed on towards the south in its work of resistance.

The task of dislodging the enemy from the high country cut by the Ancre had seemed an impossible one, and he was left in comparatively peaceful occupation of it for nearly two years. During that time he constructed defences with an elaboration never previously conceived. The future was to show how elaborate those defences were—the villages and woods, themselves bristling fortresses, that formed part of or lay immediately behind them to form yet other systems of defence, the winding dug-outs thirty feet under the ground, the concrete machine-gun emplacements and trench-mortar positions, and the miniature forts that defied artillery.

Whilst the enemy was content to remain quiet for the time being in these formidable entrenchments, he was very active in another part of the line. Verdun was being heavily pressed by him, and the French longed for some diversion of his mighty strength. To cause that diversion an attack was at this time determined on against the line so long immune north of the Somme. So the Australian soldiers who had fretted on the sands of Egypt with impatience to participate in the war in France before its finish, had apparently come in time for its real beginning.

At 7.30 on the morning of the first day of July, the great diversion—the first battle of the Somme—commenced. The British main attack was made from that part of its front which extended from Maricourt north of the Somme to a point about a mile north of Beaumont Hamel. The French forces at the same time engaged the enemy both north and south of the Somme. For a week previous to the assault the heaviest artillery fire had been directed against the enemy's defences. The infantry's advance to them on the 1st was preceded by an hour's concentrated bombardment. Some progress was made by the French on the first day's battle as well as by the extreme right wing of the British. North of this any initial success was not maintained, and by nightfall the assaulting troops to the most northern point of the front of attack were forced back to their original trenches. The high ground around Thiepval and further north had proved too formidable an obstacle. On that part of the front any further attempt at advance was for the time being abandoned, and the line there entrusted to General Gough. General Rawlinson, under whom the Australians afterwards achieved such success, proceeded with the attack and immediately set about developing such progress as he had made during the first day on the British right wing.

As a first step to its subsequent success the British attack was limited to a front of six miles. It is a strong testimony to the severity of the task, that after four days' fighting on this limited front the attack had only penetrated to a depth of one mile. In the face of its difficulties and of the limitations of the tactics of those days, this was rightly considered a great achievement.

This fighting was directed towards the north. Pozières lay near the eastern summit of the impregnable ridge, against which attack from the west had so signally failed. Rawlinson, however, was gradually pressing towards it from a southern and south-eastern direction. The advance of a mile during the first four days' fighting was at a rate of speed not sustained in the subsequent advance on the ridge, whose possession had become for the time being the great objective of the British in the Somme battle. Repeatedly were weary troops relieved and fresh troops brought to the assault. Yards of ground were gained and lost and regained. Only towards the end of July was the village of Pozières cleared of the enemy. Even then the highest part of the ridge, which lay north of the village, seemed as unattainable as ever. Thiepval still lay secure and menacing on its western side.

It was at this stage of the struggle for Pozières ridge and as one of many Australian units sharing in that struggle, that the 48th Battalion played its part in the battle of the Somme. Shortly after the capture of Pozières, it was on its way through Albert to do battle with the enemy for the higher altitude of the coveted ridge. The Battalion bivouaced for the night some two miles north-east of Albert, at a place known on the war map as Tara Hill. From its high ground the men could watch an intense bombardment by our artillery. The whole valley beneath them was lit up by blinding flashes of fire. The big guns thundered all around them. The monster howitzer at Albert every now and then fired its massive shell, which travelled slowly over their heads with the noise of a passing train. Near to the ridge the field-batteries constantly barked. Great volumes of smoke swept along the valley, whilst the air was filled with acrid-smelling fumes. It was the night of the 4th of August, and another attack was being made on the ridge above them by Australian troops.

Next day the operation order was issued, that told them what their task should be on the ridge, which they had seen burn like a Vesuvius on the preceding night. The substance of the order was briefly contained in one part of the instructions stating that the ground which had been gained was to be held at all costs. That evening they set out for their post. The path they followed was known at different parts by as many names, names which appeared and disappeared from the trench maps of the day, but which are deeply engraven on the memories of those who survived the course and end of that brief journey. Moving in single file and at intervals, platoon followed platoon up through Sausage Valley where the cookers of many Australian battalions were ranged like the stalls at a country fair; around the angle appropriately called Casualty Corner; along the Sunken Road and then stuck close to the comparative safety of Pioneer Trench. Near the junction of Pioneer Trench with Copse Avenue was the Chalk Pit, and there "D" Company left the column to take up a position in reserve. The other companies continued along Copse Avenue till Tramway Trench was reached. At Tramway Trench "B" and "C" Companies moved yet forward to do first shift on the main work of the Battalion.

The work consisted in relieving the unit holding O.G. 1 and O.G. 2, names of tragic reminiscence, that represented on the war map trenches which had been captured on the previous night. Their capture had cost the unit heavily, so heavily as to make its relief necessary as soon as darkness should come to render relief possible. The new garrison could find but little protection in their gaping walls. These had been wrecked and battered by our own artillery in the original attack on them. They were now subject to the fire of the enemy who knew the line of them only too accurately. But those trenches were to be defended "at all costs." To secure this defence much work was necessitated and well outlined beforehand, not only of active defence with the rifle and Lewis gun, but equally important work with the spade to make the rifle and Lewis gun effective or possible.

Use was to be made of the large shell-holes in front of O.G. 2. They were to be scooped out and put in a rough state of defence as strong-points to meet the enemy half way in any attempt he made against the trenches. These outposts were to be manned during the night by Lewis gun teams. Their garrisons were to steal out to them under cover of the darkness and return to O.G. 2 before dawn. Strong fighting patrols were to work between them. Digging was to go on continually in both trenches, that they might be made to afford more protection against the enemy's fire.

The relief did not work out according to programme. The two companies got as far as O.G. 1, and positions were relieved there; but the most difficult part of the task lay in finding O.G. 2. Scouting parties went forward on the right and on the left of the Battalion front. There was no answering shout from the trench ahead to give them guidance in the black darkness. Those on the right at last saw a great mound but a short distance in front. They knew it must be what remained of a windmill that had been given to them as a landmark. They had indeed already crossed over O.G. 2, no longer recognisable or of use as a trench; so there in front of the windmill they selected a position and constructed a strong-point, by means of which they continued to hold this wing of the Battalion front. The party on the left fared better, for there the trench was in parts deep and well dug. The silence of its garrison was soon explained when it was found that all were either dead or badly wounded.

That night the Battalion was finally in position about 11 o'clock; not the Battalion as it left Tara Hill a few hours previously, but a Battalion which had already suffered heavy casualties. Throughout the whole evening the terrible drum-fire of the enemy had been incessant. It still continued with unabated fury. Men who afterwards had experience of many enemy barrages ever recalled that bombardment as the most remarkable, remarkable not only for its intensity but for its long continuity and local concentration. All through the night of the 5th, all through the 6th it lasted, a great impersonal horror, until noon on the 7th, when it abated so suddenly that one felt as if the world had just been freed from the influence of some foul and demoniac oppression.

In the front trenches were men digging for their lives. Shrapnel burst over their heads. High-explosive shells stove in their wretched parapets. The wounded with the parching thirst of hemorrhage upon them called piteously for water. Ever and anon rang out that weird cry of the trenches "Stretcher-bearers wanted!" Less and pitifully less became the number of those who dug.

There was a communication sap leading from Tramway Trench to the jumping-off trench used in the preceding

"By that route came back the wounded. . . . . .
Ever did the German artillery play on it, taking toll of all its traffic, of runners, ration-carriers, stretcher-bearers, wounded."

attack, and for some distance beyond it. But a great part of it had been rendered useless for its purpose by the heavy shell-fire. The immediate approach to the front trenches was made over open ground subject to a withering fire. Along the shallow sap, over the open ground, rations and ammunition had to be carried. By that route came back the wounded, some carried, some walking, some struggling along in agonies of torture. Ever did the German artillery play on it taking toll of all its traffic, of runners, ration-carriers, stretcher-bearers, wounded. The grey fog of the morning mercifully concealed from enemy eyes the stretcher-bearers, on their mournful journey to and fro between the fatal line and Tramway Trench. But the fog availed not against the shells that required no sight. Time and again was enacted the climax of tragedy, when sufferers and their succourers were hurtled to simultaneous death.

It was thought that the sustained heavy shelling could have but one ending, a counter-attack of the enemy. The Battalion commander therefore made all preparations for it on the evening of the 6th. The company that had been in reserve now took over the trenches O.G. 1 and O.G. 2 from the very reduced companies that were holding them. The support company was still kept in close support, for a bitter lesson had been learned as to the inadvisability of crowding men in the trenches. It was rightly considered better to risk a temporary set-back than to make casualties certain.

At 5 o'clock the next morning the expected counter-attack was made. The S.O.S. was immediately sent up for artillery protection. Messages were also sent to the rear by Pigeon Service and by runners, for in that area of concentrated shelling no one could trust the telephone wires. But before these messages brought their redeeming help, the first wave of the advancing enemy appeared over the crest of the ridge. On the left side of the trench the enemy succeeded in penetrating our line, not evenly and regularly but in small groups here and there.

The position for a time was a dangerous one and it looked as if the Germans would not only regain the ground but also make easy capture of a few prisoners. But with the unit on the left flank of the 48th was a soldier who had a good head for an emergency, Jacka V.C. of the 14th. With a small body of men he cleverly attacked the enemy from the rear even as two platoons of the support company of the 48th rushed forward. The Germans, so lately enjoying a partial success, were thus made prisoners. Just then down came our artillery barrage. It caught great numbers of the enemy who were lying on the other side of the ridge, waiting to exploit the success of the preceding waves in the advance. The havoc wrought among the enemy was very great, and they made no further attempts to regain the much disputed trenches.

After that terrible ordeal the same work of getting away the wounded recommenced, the same congestion of the narrow sap at Battalion headquarters where was the medical officer with his many helpers. Along that narrow trench the wounded lay whilst one dreaded the tragedy that a chance shell might cause among them.

Even as those wounded were being taken away one of those tragedies of ill-chance was being enacted further down the sap. Some details of the two companies of the 48th which had been relieved on the preceding evening, were gathered around a Battalion cooker in the cold raw morning waiting for a drink of tea. A shell fell near the cooker and killed twenty-six men immediately and wounded sixteen. The memory of this disaster remained long with men in the 48th. The great destruction of human life caused by one shell and the hard ill-fortune overwhelming the victims who had already survived so much, were the outstanding features that made it an incident not easily forgotten in the Battalion.

There was no possibility of relieving the small garrison until darkness should come to cover their movements, so the men settled down to another day. Still the shells rained upon them and still their numbers grew less, until noon when the intense bombardment suddenly abated. Then it was these survivors had some hope of getting away from that death-trap. For the remainder of the day they were in comfort by contrast with the conditions they had hitherto been experiencing.

At night relief came. It was not a Battalion that marched out of the trenches but more like a jaded, tired, worn-out working-party making its way to the rear before dawn after a night spent in digging a jumping-off trench for some fresh advance, but presenting such a picture of war-worn weariness as no working-party has ever shown. One by one the men filed down Pioneer Trench along the sunken road and back again through Sausage Gully.

What had they done since they went up that gully two nights previously ? Apparently very little, it looks but very little on the war map. Their work had been to hold Old German Trench No. 1 and Old German Trench No. 2 at all costs. They delivered over those trenches to the relieving unit. They had done their work.

Chapter VII.

POZIERES RIDGE—THE WINDMILL.

ON the night of the 7th the men slept at the foot of Sausage Gully, slept undisturbed by the roar of the artillery, and heedless of the noisy reveille sounded by the guns as they began the intense bombardment which always preceded the dawn. The sun at last dissipated the heavy morning fog which was then prevalent, and its rays beat down upon their exposed bivouac. Still they slept that heavy sleep which follows a night of relief from a hard vigil in the trenches, when the breakfast-hour passes unheeded, when " cook-house" is shouted at mid-day and men wearily raise themselves to swear at the cooks and again roll over in slumber, when there is little or no assorting, but officers and men lie in one inert mass, and the quartermaster and transport-officer come up from the rear to supply the only show of activity in the silent bivouac.

Some stir first began around the improvised orderly-room. Lists were being consulted and casualties reckoned. Casualties were already known to be heavy, and their summing-up made a sad total. Of officers there were six killed —Dyke, English barrister, traveller, author, and young Walters, and Jack Cosson, a cheery, shrewd old bookmaker of the West, and Richardson, and Ottaway and Hawke. Fourteen officers were wounded. Ninety-eight of other ranks had been killed and seventy-six were officially reported as missing, which could but mean death in that grim fight where tally of its many fatal events was impossbile, for the

Battalion lost no prisoners to the enemy. Four hundred and four men had been wounded, thus bringing the unit's casualties in officers and men to the awful total of five hundred and ninety-eight. What remained of the effective strength of the Battalion made a very small party.

The men rested throughout the 8th and again on the 9th of August, recounting incidents of their adventure, recalling to one another how this man and that man was killed, and often interspersing their reminiscences with vows of vengeance for the loss of this pal or that pal. Some wrote letters to people at home to give them the too premature assurance that they were quite safe. Others wrote offering honest sympathy to the relatives of comrades killed, narrating such details as they cared to describe of those last moments, knowledge of which is so much sought after by bereaved parents.

In their present position there could be little regular training. The Lewis gun, however, had proved a good friend in the trenches ; and as casualties had occurred among the gunners many new hands were told off for immediate instruction to fill the vacant places, and to form a useful emergency reserve.

With the reaction so pronounced in men whose routine is war, life again became normal. Some began to growl again about their rations, to curse the Army Service Corps, to quarrel with one another on a dozen different subjects and agree only on the merits of their own Battalion. That agreement, always easily arrived at in every unit, had been strengthened by their two days' experience on Pozières Ridge, and was further enhanced by the following special order read to them on the morning of the 10th of August :

SPECIAL ORDER OF THE DAY.

By Lt.-Col. R. L. Leane, D.S.O., M.C.

10/8/1916.

After a short but strenuous period in the front line of trenches, the 48th Battalion has been withdrawn to rest and re-organise, but not to relax. The Battalion in forty-eight hours has won for itself a name that every officer, every N.C.O., and every man should deem it his sacred duty to uphold, a name for unflinching courage and stoical endurance. It is true that in those two stern days, many of our comrades were lost to us, but let it not be thought that their sacrifice was in vain. We were given a most important trust : we were called upon to hold at all costs the ground won by the preceding Battalion : and we held it, in spite of the most determined efforts of the enemy to regain the position.

The following copy of a special Order issued by General von Bulow which was taken from a German prisoner, bears witness to the importance placed by the enemy on the position of the Pozières Plateau :—

"At any price the Pozières Plateau (Hill 60) must be recovered, for if it remained in the hands of the British, it would give them an important advantage. Attacks will be made by successive waves 80 yards apart. Troops which first reach the Plateau must hold on until reinforced, whatever their losses. Any officer or man who fails to resist to the death on the ground won will be immediately court-martialled."

We were subjected to a bombardment of an intensity that has not been surpassed by any previous bombardment in the history of the war, until our ranks were most appallingly depleted. This was followed by an infantry attack the first waves of which, although in places penetrating our line, were driven out and back, leaving a large proportion of their number dead or prisoners in our hands. The succeeding waves were caught in our artillery barrage, which followed most rapidly on our call for retaliation ; large numbers of the enemy were accounted for in the valley below our lines, and the attack was finally broken up and abandoned.

To the medical section special praise belongs. Our medical staff and stretcher-bearers had to perform much of their work in the open, under heavy fire. Through their fearlessness and untiring zeal, when we were at last relieved from the trenches we had brought in not only our wounded but also those who had been left by the Brigade which preceded us.

The General Officer commanding 1st A.N.Z.A.C., the G.O.C. 4th Division, and the G.O.C. 12th Aust. Inf. Bde. have all been pleased to express their appreciation of the good work achieved by this Battalion, and the commanding officer wishes to say that he is deeply proud of his command.

As we have begun so we must continue, so that the Battalion shall always have a name for endurance, for courage and for stern determination. See to it, men, that your N.C.O.'s and Officers have your loyal support; that new reinforcements who come to build up our strength again are made to know what standard of soldiership is required of them; and that the esprit de corps, which comes from dangers shared and battles fought together, is maintained and fostered as long as the Battalion shall last.

(Signed) B. B. LEANE, Capt.
Adjutant 48th Battalion.

One thing was suggested by the order, as well as by their continued stay so close to the battle-front. Another turn in the trenches was evidently imminent. Next day it was definitely announced that during the night they should return to the defence of the same ground which they had left only three days previously.

Their ranks had been much thinned, and it seemed a risky experiment to entrust such a strenuous defence to those weary men. But the Colonel had no will in the matter, and indeed he preferred this manner of attempting the task with a third of the men he had previously employed.

He had made careful reconnaissance of the area previous to the Battalion's first occupation of the line. He foresaw the havoc which the concentrated shelling would work among a platoon, a company, a battalion caught whilst making its way through those congested saps, and what little chance of avoiding casualties existed for men who should be crowded in the inadequate trenches. Strongly did he insist that it was better to risk a temporary penetration of the line for one strenuous moment, than to suffer passively and continuously from the congested front presented to the enemy's shell-fire.

Those were the days, however, when close formation in defence was as popular with us as was close formation in attack popular with the enemy. Then a unit went into the line in all the pride of its full fighting strength, and along the crowded saps many a battalion paid dearly before the lesson of other tactics was learned. Later on some five hundred rifles represented a unit's strength in the line, whilst one-third of the Battalion's effective strength was prudently kept out of action.

When on the morning of the 12th the Battalion was again in O.G. 1 and O.G. 2 there was no congestion. The number of men was small enough for the work to be done, which kept all hands busy. Tramway Trench was further improved as well as the communication-sap that ran towards the front trenches. The attempts to improve O.G. 1 and O.G. 2 were not so successful, for these trenches were an easy mark to the enemy and shells constantly undid the work expended on them.

But during this term in the line the shelling of the position was light in comparison with what they had previously experienced. Occasionally it was very intense, as on the 13th and again on the night of the 14th. The old Windmill was still a storm centre, and shells from our guns that fell short were landing on it as frequently as were the shells of the enemy. During their third evening in the line, the enemy shelled the trenches so heavily that it was thought he intended to make another counter-attack, but our artillery brought prompt retaliation to bear upon the other side of the crest. This eased the situation somewhat but not before Captain Evans and a number of other ranks were killed. On the preceding day Lieutenant Law had been killed, an officer whose

"Its surroundings peopled by so many of Australia's dead, the site of the old Windmill has since been sacred to Australian soldiers. But it was an unlucky landmark and a thing of ill omen in those days . . . ."

fate was a hard one, for he had just been transferred to the Battalion after spending a strenuous time in the trenches with his previous unit.

Next morning the 48th was relieved by another Australian unit, and stole away from the trenches in the dense fog of the early morning. The second term in the line had been of three days' duration and the casualty list was a comparatively small one. Two officers had been killed and twenty-one of other ranks, whilst three of other ranks were reported missing and sixty-three wounded. It is true they had sustained no such heavy shelling and no counter-attack, but the shelling was continuous and at times intense; and although the casualty list was indeed long enough, its contrast with that of the previous term was an instructive as well as a happy one.

Near to the Windmill, whose name seemed to be on all men's lips during those fierce days, lay the dead of the 48th. They were buried with what brief ceremony the circumstances allowed. Some were buried where they had fallen, for the living have the first claim and the transport of the wounded was in itself all too difficult. Others were buried near the Chalk Pit, where something of the uniformity of peace time was given to their last resting-place. Later on, when conditions allowed it, more permanent organization was introduced into the great irregular burying-ground that contained the dead of so many Australian units. On the slope of the Ridge was erected a monument to the many known and unknown Australians who slept there. When nearly two years afterwards the tide of battle, which had receded far from the Ridge, again swept over the land enveloping Pozières and the country around, the enemy, so unaccustomed to respect anything sacred or profane, nevertheless respected that monument to the memory of the men who so withstood him. Its surroundings peopled by so many of Australia's dead, the site of the old Windmill has since been sacred to Australian soldiers. But it was an unlucky landmark and a thing of ill omen in those days, and the men of the 48th gladly turned their backs on it.

Away down to Albert they went, that 15th day of August, on to the old brick-fields again, where they bivouaced for the night unmindful of the weather. Next morning they started at 7 o'clock, and, marching through a downpour of rain to Warloy, arrived there drenched but happy to see civilian people once more. There they rested for the remainder of the day and during the next day, but on the morning of the 18th they again turned towards the friendly West and reached Hérissart. Next day they were early on the march, keeping to the inferior roads away from the main highways of military traffic. Still it rained till their clothes were sodden and their boots oozed mud, rained whilst they marched again into Berteaucourt and felt they had at last come home.

The return to Berteaucourt was a real home-coming, though a sad one. Those kindly French people turned out to greet the old Battalion which had grown so familiar during its brief sojourn among them. But when they saw that small party looking so ill-used by war and weather, and understood it was all that remained of the imposing unit that had marched away, such a wailing chorus of grief and sympathy went up from them as embarrassed even the usually casual soldiers. Old men mournfully shook their heads and murmured something about " soixante-dix." Old women and young women wept. Many merged with the column unminded by the officers, to enquire the fate of their numerous friends, of " Jack," of " Monsieur George," of " le Sergeant."

At Berteaucourt the Battalion settled for a week in happy forgetfulness of the horrors of Pozières Ridge.

Chapter VIII.

POZIERES RIDGE—MOUQUET FARM.

FROM Berteaucourt the Battalion set out on the 23rd of August, marching eastward to Talmas. Thence on the following day eastward still to Rubempré. Sodden with rain, the men reached Vadincourt on the 26th and there camped in a neighbouring wood.

Next day General Birdwood paid one of those flying visits to the Brigade, which no pressure of business ever prevented his making when any of his various units had done something that deserved appreciation, or had lost good comrades and needed condolence or encouragement. He addressed the men gathered around him in the wood, and spoke appreciatively of the good work they had done. In addition he broadly hinted of an opportunity of doing even greater work in the near future.

The men liked General Birdwood, liked the trim, neat figure so plain and business-like in dress. They liked his incisive, accentless voice, his interest in them individually, in their home-lives, the different parts of Australia they came from, and all the little ways in which he showed his anxiety to have their friendship as well as their service. Especially they liked him for his unostentatious manner of coming among them, leaving behind all the following of " red-tabbed Johnnies" on whom the digger looked not with a kindly eye. Sometimes they swore roundly against him for his high opinion of them, imputing to that the frequent use made of them for the severest tasks; but their grievance had in it more of fondness than of resentment.

On the following day the march was resumed towards Albert where a halt was made for dinner, and that evening the Battalion took up a position in reserve at La Boiselle, a ruined village some two miles along the main road between Albert and Bapaume. The men were again within the range of the guns, but only a few shells fell in the area occupied by them.

A definite task had been allotted to the Battalion, but on the afternoon of the 30th all the arrangements were cancelled. The Battalion commander got hurried orders to reconnoitre the front line at Mouquet Farm, with a view to relieving that night the troops holding it. So he set out on the long and necessarily circuitous route that led to that part of the line, taking with him his company commanders. Their journey was a tedious and a harrowing one. The communication-sap was full of dead men and of dying men who had to be left there to die, or who were with great difficulty pulled out of the enveloping mud and laid on the bank to die. Stretcher-bearers struggled through the mud with wounded who had a better chance of surviving the journey to the rear.

Along this avenue of dead and dying the officers slowly made their way, delayed by passing stretchers, delayed by the necessity of lending a hand where pity might well make military duty forgotten, and delayed not a little by the weight of their own fatigue. When finally they arrived at their destination much was to be done, much information to be got, a Battalion headquarters to be found that would be in closer touch with the line, a medical aid-station to be established that should lessen the hardship of the wounded and the labour of the stretcher-bearers.

These are some of the duties of officers who go forward to the line to map the course and define positions for their Battalion. The carrying out of these duties obviously entails work of far-reaching importance. Sometimes the work is well done, sometimes it is done indifferently. The manner in which it is done has often a very decisive effect on the subsequent casualty-list of the Battalion. In this case it was not done indifferently; but its doing required much time and the work had begun late, so that there was no possibility of those officers returning by the same path in time to start again with the Battalion on its journey from La Boiselle.

A message was therefore sent to La Boiselle, and at 8 o'clock that night the Battalion started for the trenches. Its destination was but another part of Pozières Ridge, the *ferme du Mouquet*, lying about a mile north-west of the village of Pozières. The distance between La Boiselle and Mouquet Farm does not look formidable on the map. But the crow's flight is not the route which a Battalion would have dared to take in that dangerous area. By many a cautious detour crept the unit before the long, winding communication-sap was reached which led to the front line.

This sap was the well-trodden track in every Battalion sector, wherein is concentrated all the activity between the front line and its immediate rear in the infantry zone of battle. It is a track that is well known to the Battalion runners ever going to and fro, who from there onwards proceed with caution if "going up" the line or with casual confidence if "going down" the line. Well known also to the signallers, those birds of the night who are ever tinkering with its many strands of telephone-wire. And well known to the stretcher-bearers, who further congest it with their pitiful traffic that must not be delayed.

All that normal congestion existed on the night of the 30th, when the men of the 48th struggled along it towards Mouquet Farm. It had rained almost constantly during many days past, rained whilst the Battalion was on the way to Albert, rained whilst it lay around the ruins of La Boiselle, and on this night the rain came down in one unbroken sheet of water. The sap was in some parts a river. The water lay deep and men plunged into it till it was above their knees and lapping at their flanks. In other parts the trench ran over higher ground where the water was shallow, but the mud was deep, so deep that the men clung to the sides of the trench to assist deliberately each step they took. Sometimes a youngster fell, a weakling, weak with the immaturity of youth and fretfully protested his inability to proceed further; whilst a stronger comrade swore at him for his weakness and pulled him free of the mud, only to find that the effort had imprisoned himself. And those at the tail end of the column waited for clearance knowing not what might be befalling their comrades further ahead, waited in the gathering darkness when shells seem to fall so closely, and blunted sense of direction gives such false judgment of their location.

It was a fortunate thing that the Battalion was at this time very low in strength. In fact it had received no reinforcements to make up the great losses sustained on its two previous ventures on the ridge, and now mustered only about three hundred rifles. It was therefore a comparatively small body of men that made the passage of the river of mud which led to Mouquet Farm. So they had few casualties on the way up. Some men did not reach the end of the journey till late on the following morning, and it was a very small party that relieved the unit then holding the line.

The Battalion so diminished in numbers had a comparatively quiet time from the enemy, for although the shelling was at times intense the Germans had apparently no intention of attempting an attack. Very grim fighting had taken place there but a short time before, and there was promise of heavy fighting in the near future. In fact the principal work of the 48th and other units of the Brigade then holding the sector, was to prepare the way for an attack to be made by the Brigade which should relieve them. The front line was not a trench but a maze of old German trenches that seemed impossible of defence. A new trench was cut through this maze, shortening considerably the stretch of country to be held, whilst a new communication-trench was constructed that facilitated connection with the rear. All this work

". . . . the passage of the river of mud which led to Mouquet Farm. . . . And those at the tail end of the column waited for clearance . . . . . waited in the gathering darkness when shells seem to fall so closely, and blunted sense of direction gives such false judgment of their location."

made a very big demand on the small number of men with which the unit was holding the line.

One rather interesting feature of this term at Mouquet Farm, was the almost friendly spirit that existed between our troops and the enemy. Such was the nature of the country, that the opposite trenches could not fail to command a very good view of any conspicuous movement on our side. But from the first morning our men went into the trenches, the white flag was in constant use by both sides when wounded had to be removed. The Australians approached the German trenches unharmed, to remove wounded men of whose presence the enemy often acquainted them. A similar freedom was accorded the enemy. Both sides, however, were rather keen to prevent any abuse of the liberty. They were particularly suspicious of officers observing dispositions under the pretext of looking for wounded.

On the first morning of the Battalion's occupation of the line, Colonel Leane was making his usual round of the front when he suddenly found himself but a few yards from two German soldiers. He immediately decided that he had lost his way and had wandered into the German lines, not a very difficult thing to do in that network of trenches. He kept himself concealed, and awaited his chance to run in a direction which he hoped should bring him to his own lines. He had not gone far before he discovered himself in a trench occupied by men of the 46th Battalion. They were able to explain the close proximity of the two Germans, who had been so casual in their manner as to give the Colonel the impression that he was right behind the German front line. One of the Germans was an officer speaking English fluently, and he had come to look for the body of his brother who had been recently killed there. But whether his story was true or false, soldiers are wont to make a great difference between a dead man and a wounded man. It is not prudent to have a unit's trenches and dispositions overlooked by an enemy, for such a slight consideration as the proper burial of that enemy's brother. So the officer was allowed but a short time to go back to his own lines, his sense of fraternal duty having nearly cost him his life.

A short time after this incident Colonel Leane met a British officer in his Battalion sector who was unknown to him. The Colonel's previous encounter with the German officer, who spoke good English, might have made him inclined to be suspicious. Moreover the individual in his path was most correctly dressed, he was well groomed, his clothes were innocent of mud. Colonel Leane was not in a mood to tolerate a clean and fastidiously-dressed officer in his trenches. In his opinion the interloper must be a Staff-officer, an idler, or a spy; and in any case he was unwelcome. To be a Staff-officer or even an idler is not a criminal offence, so the Colonel was wont to get over the difficulty by treating all such strangers as spies until proved otherwise. This unknown one protested that he belonged to artillery, that he was a liason officer, but he did not remember to what infantry unit he was temporarily attached. He gave several unsatisfactory answers to several reasonable and unreasonable questions, was put under arrest and immediately marched back to the rear under an escort that gave him little chance of avoiding the mud. Of course the poor stray was not a spy, his battery readily identified him, but resolved to make him display a more workmanlike appearance and memory for the future.

The Battalion got a speedy release from Mouquet Farm and made its way back to Albert. It was destined to be free from the struggle of Pozières Ridge for several weeks. But the days it had already spent on the ridge and the grim experiences it there endured, left their mark on the unit throughout the rest of its career. The 48th was one of the new formations, and although some of its officers and many of its men had seen service on Gallipoli, the vast majority had no further experience of war than that gained in the peaceful trenches of Fleurbaix. Some of the officers in the unit, as in all such units formed at the same time, were not men that nature ever intended to endure the hard things of such a hard war. Some of them were elderly men who had seen service in other fields, but who had to come to Pozières to learn that the years had stolen from them their vigour and endurance. Others were good officers in training their men, conscientious fellows in looking after them, officers who gave fair promise of being good leaders when the real test of leadership should come. Pozières found them wanting. The trial was in some cases pathetic as the trial of the inculpably inefficient often is ; in some cases it was ludicrous ; but always the verdict was unquestioned and unquestionable.

Pozières also tried the strong and proved their strength, and henceforth the comparatively new Battalion knew what manner of men it desired for officers or for its rank and file. Many of its strong men had been killed though not conquered by Pozières, and their spirit was ever after held up to the personnel of the Battalion as the ideal at which all ranks should aim. Its strong men who survived Pozières became henceforth the keepers of its honour.

This spirit of the unit which it gained from the struggle on the ridge was the best and indeed its only reward. No adequate recognition could come to the Battalion for that kind of fighting. Great honours are not given for a Pozières. There you had none of the glamour of advance, none of the glory of success. There you had only grim holding-on to ground that was all but untenable. There you had only sustaining of counter-attacks that were all but irresistible. But the bodies of dead comrades strewn along its shallow trenches ; the prostrate figures that lay wounded in the crowded sap which served as an aid-post : these bore their testimony to the heroism that was shown and—it would almost seem—wasted on Pozières Ridge.

Chapter IX.

IN FLANDERS.

THE Battalion left Albert next day and went to Warloy, where it spent the night, afterwards going on to Hérissart. From there it proceeded to Beauval, where the men discussed the probability of their going up north for an attack in the Ypres salient. For just then the 4th Australian Division was entraining for Flanders, and the 48th Battalion leaving Doullens on the 8th detrained at Proven that night about 12 o'clock. From there it marched to Connaught Camp near Popperinghe, where about a week was spent.

At Popperinghe there was a picture-show, and although their camp lay some distance from the village the men missed no opportunity of visiting it. It was indeed a commonplace enough entertainment, but to the men who had just come through stern days on Pozières Ridge that third-rate picture-show was a source of riotous joy.

Their first visit to this relaxation of peace-time days gave the diggers an opportunity of doing something they dearly loved, "putting a rough one up on the old man." The Battalion commander was marching at their head, and the small party was swinging along easily and with all the appearance of being out on pleasure bent. They interested a soldier of another Australian unit who was casually regarding them as they passed, and who finally hailed them with "Hello! you blokes, where are you going to?" Readily did the answer come back to him, "Oh dad is bringing us to the movies."

The 4th Australian Division together with the other Australian Divisions was now in Flanders. Rumour was false, however, in the 48th Battalion, when it said that the Australians were being sent to the north for an attack in the Ypres salient. During the period starting with the Somme battle, all the northern sector of the British front had remained comparatively quiet, except for the attack made at Fleurbaix in the middle of July when the 5th Australian Division was set its hard task. The policy in this sector was to make small local raids on the enemy trenches, with the purpose of keeping enemy forces employed whilst the attack proceeded on the Somme, and at the same time obtaining valuable information as to the constitution and disposition of the opposing forces. This policy was to be maintained by the Australians.

On the 16th of the month there was a sports meeting, the first organised sports which the Battalion had held since coming to France. A feature now and henceforth of such meetings was the special competition for Lewis gunners of the unit. The record which a successful competitor would hold for stripping a Lewis gun, reassembling its parts, and remedying stoppages, excited the same popular interest as the pedigree of a racehorse or the contests of a boxer.

It was the strangest feature of the life of the campaign, this quick transition from a bloody, smoking Pozières to a green, laughing sports-field. No contest in any stadium was ever more exciting than a "jam-fight." No picture show ever more thrilling than one in a wrecked school-room. No interest more absorbing than that excited by the crudest stage-properties of a Battalion entertainment. No Marathon with more spirit of competition than a race run in grey Army socks. No Cup favourite more discussed than the chances of a transport mule.

The frolic of those gatherings was so different to the " cheery and bright ' pose which the imaginative journalist attributes to the trenches. The humour of war is but a home-made fiction, or at best a hysterical counterfeit which good soldiers contemned. The laughter of a mule-race behind the lines was as real as war itself.

Some would explain the brightness of this light side of war as nature's reaction; the recuperative work of nature filling out again those drawn features which war had robbed of the roundness of youth, smoothing the lines of those prematurely old faces, bringing back the light of boyhood to those haggard eyes. Perhaps it was so. Others would say it was of the race, it was British, it was the heart of our boys ; and there again is arid journalism.

There seemed something far more solemn in it than any of these things. It seemed that away up there in the trenches the world was stripped of all things complex, and men stood naked and alone with the great mysteries of life and death. In those trenches where they saw so many die, they too had died to the world of teeming cities. When they came down they were as men born again, no longer men but children despite their tired eyes and aged faces, and like children easily happy.

Two days after holding its sports meeting the Battalion moved to a camp near Renninghelst, and on the 21st to the village of La Clytte. From this place two of the other Battalions of the Brigade went forward and relieved Canadian troops holding the front line.

The Brigade sector lay some miles south of the Ypres salient, but the ruined town itself was only a short distance away, and was then little troubled by the enemy's guns. So members of the Battalion availed themselves of the opportunity to visit the place whose name was so much associated with the early stages of the war. They had also an opportunity of seeing their comrades in other Australian Divisions engaged in the same sector.

The 48th relieved the 46th Battalion about a week later, and although the men's description of the sector as " a rest

camp in the front line" may have been too flattering, their
new conditions afforded a pleasant contrast to those they had
experienced on the Somme. The line of defence was composed of the barricade trenches that prevailed in this northern
part, and bore the signs of many months of weather and many
attempts at repair. One could look from them over to
Wytschaete, whilst a little further to the south lay Messines,
both of them villages with which the Battalion was to make
closer acquaintance the following year.

But this term in the front area was not one of unbroken
rest. The enemy's guns had the range to a nicety of the
long-stationary defence line, and his slow, clumsy "rumjars" made up for their inaccuracy by the wide area of their
destructiveness. There the two lines ran very close to each
other, at some places being only eighty yards apart, and
offered a good opportunity to both sides for the use of trenchmortars. Our Stokes guns were very active during those
days and evidently provoked the enemy's wrath, for he used
several times during the day subject the area to a few minutes'
intense shelling. They were thought to have excited his
curiosity also, for one night he concentrated all his fire on a
section of the front, and after easily breaking down its wretched
barricades attempted to raid it with a view to finding one of
the novel guns.

Now and then casualties were sustained in this manner,
and those onslaughts usually left much work to be done in
repairing the trenches. One communication-sap known as
Poppy Lane used to get special attention from the enemy's
machine-guns, and parts of it had to be roofed in with sandbags for protection against his frequent enfilading. An
immediate support line some two hundred yards behind the
front line was completed during this term, and the sand-bag
shelters in which the Battalion was accommodated required
constant repair or rebuilding.

These tasks of repair and consolidation made up the usual
routine of continuous employment that prevails on a quiet

front. It was whilst so engaged that the first referendum on Australian conscription was taken.

Meanwhile the policy which prevailed in the northern sector was continued, and the enemy kept busy by raids on his trenches. The raiding was conducted by parties sometimes numbering not more than sixty men. They were specially trained for the operation beforehand, making several rehearsals of its details. Two such raids were made at this time by other Battalions of the Brigade, when the inevitable artillery retaliation of the enemy caused some casualties in the 48th, one officer and several of other ranks being killed.

After about a fortnight in the front line the Battalion was again withdrawn to Brigade reserve, where a party was immediately selected to train for one of these raids. But in the midst of much preparation it was notified that the Brigade would be relieved by English troops, and on the 22nd of October the Battalion marched away from the area.

During this term in the north the Battalion, like other Australian units in the same sector, had had time to get much needed reinforcements and to organise its resources. Counting all ranks its strength was now nearly seven hundred when on the 26th of the month it again entrained for the Somme area.

Chapter X.

THE WINTER OF 1916-1917.

THE Battalion again journeying towards the south was returning to places already made quite familiar during its previous term of fighting on the Somme.

On the morning of the 27th of October the men detrained at Longpré, and from there marched to Villers-Sous-Ailly, two days later to Bertincourt and on the following day to Vaux. This latter, a pleasant district, was very suitable for training, and officers and men discussed the possibility of the winter being spent in it. For some argued that the powers that be had too much regard for the lives and lungs of Australians to submit them to the rigours of winter in the trenches. But three days later they were again marching to Flesselles, and on the following morning a long column of motor lorries carried the Battalion to the village of Dernancourt.

Dernancourt was even then partly in ruins, and the limited accommodation it afforded as well as the rain and mud of an early winter, made it a very wretched place. Here the daily waste of the Battalion through sickness would in a short time have left it very much depleted in strength. Many of the men had contracted colds, and when the soldier in the field has even a slight ailment, he has little chance of getting rid of it except by treatment in hospital. He has no room to which to confine himself in pyjamas and slippers. He must go to hospital, be struck off the strength of his unit, and when he has been discharged from hospital much time elapses before he is returned. But the medical officer obviated this by establishing a small hospital within the regiment, where men could be well cared for who were only temporarily indisposed.

After a few days spent at Dernancourt the Battalion went to Fricourt, a village which was at that time levelled to the ground. From there to Switch Trench where the unit took up a position in support of the Brigade. This trench was deep in water and mud, no shelters of any kind were available, and it afforded practically no protection from shellfire. German air-craft was particularly active at that time, and in the infantryman's estimation the enemy was having everything his own way in the air. Aeroplane observation soon discovered the presence of troops in Switch Trench, with the result that the trench was heavily shelled periodically and a number of casualties inflicted.

But worse than the enemy shell-fire were the impossible conditions under which the troops were living. Their dress was fighting-order with one blanket and oil sheet, great-coats and packs having been dumped at Dernancourt. So they settled down to fight what was to be their most formidable enemy during the next five months—the winter, its rain and snow, its frost, its hunger and cold. That trench was drained and dug and re-dug. It contained no dug-outs or shelters of any kind that could protect from either shell-fire or weather, and all ranks rested during the night by lying snuggled under their waterproof sheets stretched across the trench. Parades were held frequently to inspect the men's feet, to insist on having wet feet dried, on having whale-oil rubbed into them, to see that wet socks were changed. Meals were cooked in the open trench, a practice not looked on with favour by the higher commands, for it was feared that the smoke might attract the enemy's artillery-fire. It probably did so, but the risk was more than counter-balanced by the effect on the troops of substantial hot meals.

On the night of the 18th the Battalion moved into the front line. The day before had witnessed the first of the winter's snow-storms, and all the country around was a desolate wilderness. General Glassfurd, the Brigade-commander, had already been killed in this sector, and the casualties of the preceding units though not very heavy afforded evidence of a rather lively time in the front trenches. But the men set to work and in a short time things were more tolerable than life in Switch Trench. The line now ran over high ground for the most part, and once it had been cleaned out the troops could rest in conditions which by contrast were comfortable.

But the approaches to the line were in a frightful state: they were dangerous, they were long and tedious, and therein lay the awful hardship of that term in the trenches. For those men had to be fed and fed well, if they should endure such hard conditions. And one looking back at that great struggle for existence and endurance, cannot but admire the organization which made success possible. Food had to be cooked at the ruined village of Flers nearly a mile away. Thence a hot meal was carried by fatigue-parties morning and evening. A meal carried such a distance in winter, carried in petrol-tins with blankets sewn around them to preserve their heat might not impress the average person very favourably. But one has got to be in the trenches and to share once in the good stew that can be contained in a petrol-tin, in order to understand how preferable it is to the cold Army ration. In such a manner was food carried to the troops morning and evening, whilst at 5 a.m. and 3 p.m. bovril or hot milk, to which their rum ration had been added, was stolen to them along that dangerous track. In the same way dry socks were conveyed to the front trenches every day, whilst wet socks were removed and feet dried and massaged.

A person having but a vague idea of the horrors of trench warfare in winter, or who merely reads of its hardship with an imagination little adequate to visualizing its details, might think that men thus provided for were quite happy.

So indeed they were happy, if manly and cheerful acceptance of their circumstances should be called happiness. But such were those circumstances that all the organization and labour expended were needed to make them tolerable. One remembers well other units where the same organization and labour were not shown, and their ranks were thinned by sickness before they had spent forty-eight hours in the line. The German was no longer the great enemy, it was the winter. Therefore was it that Battalion commanders whose tactics were good enough or at least harmless, were in those days promptly removed from their commands on plain questions of hot stew and dry socks.

Yet all the foresight and care expended could not entirely ward off the dread of the soldier, trench-feet. Men came over the rising ground to the medical aid-post dug into the shelter of the ridge at Grass Lane, limping painfully in boots that had to be cut from their feet to disclose the swelling and dull discolouring of incipient frost-bite. Every effort was made to check the malady, and often the sufferers were able to resume their work. Others were unable to do so, and left the trenches on the long journey to the rear. Their feet wrapped in cotton-wool, they limped along or negotiated a particularly difficult bit of ground on the shoulders of a passing digger. A weird sight presenting a sordid picture of war, weirder for the suggestion which it obtruded on the onlooker of a schoolboy game in some happy play-ground.

After eight days spent in these conditions the Battalion was relieved, the relief starting before 9 o'clock in the heavy grey fog of the November evening, and not being completed until after midnight. Then the men trailed through the slush and mud back to Mametz, which they reached early in the morning. Here they were housed in wooden huts, and the unit settled down to repair the ravages of life in the trenches.

A week later the Battalion marched back to Dernancourt, where all ranks had access to their packs which had been

". . . . trench feet. . . . . Their feet wrapped in cotton-wool, they limped along or negotiated a particularly difficult bit of ground on the shoulders of a passing digger. A weird sight presenting a sordid picture of war, weirder for the suggestion it obtruded on the onlooker of a schoolboy game in some happy play-ground."

dumped at that village three weeks previously. Little training could be done there, so great was the congestion of troops in the area. So on the 17th of December the unit entrained for Flesselles, a happy village in which the men spent their first Christmas in France. New Year's Day was celebrated in the same place by a Brigade sports meeting. The results of the various competitions, in which the Battalion led the other units of the Brigade, were duly and solemnly entered in the Battalion War Diary and on the following day the men set out to resume the sterner sport of the trenches.

From Flesselles to Franvillers, then on to Dernancourt, then to Fricourt, stopping but a night at each village, so that five days after their sports meeting at Flesselles they were again in the front line trenches at Gueudecourt. Here all the hard conditions of their first winter term in the trenches were again encountered, but encountered with even more efficiency and success. Ways and means of communicating with the front line were perhaps more difficult than before, the shortest route over which ammunition and rations had to be man-handled involving a distance of two miles. That journey was made over a dangerous and unprotected track, which could only be used between 5 o'clock in the evening and 5 o'clock in the morning. But the men stuck to this fighting against cold and hunger and wet and discomfort of every kind, just as they stuck to the fighting against German artillery in the trenches at Pozières. They endured a term of ten days in the front line before relief came to them.

There now ensued a period lasting from the middle of January until the middle of February, when the Battalion was quartered in different camps scattered over the reserve area. It was not a pleasant period in the estimation of the men. Brisbane Camp, Albury Camp, Townsville Camp, with their comfortless wooden huts like toy boats at anchor in a sea of mud, sadly belied the climate and character of the places after which they had been named.

A heavy fall of snow was soon afterwards followed by frost which lasted about three weeks. This made things much more tolerable, the men were dry and were able to enjoy themselves during the days, which were usually very pleasant. But at night the cold in those huts was a hard ordeal, for coal could not be procured and it was almost equally impossible to obtain supplies of wood.

If the discomforts of this period were distasteful to the men, not less so was the character of the work in which they were engaged. For their occupation during the day was that of making or mending roads, and whether rightly or wrongly the digger thought that those who put him to such work were scarcely playing the game. Even at this comparatively early date, he had come to look upon himself as worth preserving for front-line work only. He resented his unit being used as a Labour Battalion, and at the same time being called on when necessity arose to do the work of stormtroops. It was no satisfying retort to him, that regiments of the Guards Division also had to work at road making. For he had seen a regiment of Guards at Flers look tremulously for relief and get it after forty-eight hours; whilst he and his cobbers from the sunny south shivered in the snow and cursed their bad luck, but stuck to it doggedly for another six days.

In the middle of February the Battalion again moved to the front line, in the same area as that which was previously occupied by it. At the same time the thaw came, and the long-sustained frost was at an end. The enemy's artillery was very active, whilst his infantry were so remarkably quiet in the trenches as to arouse suspicion. So the Battalion scouts patrolled the front every night endeavouring to find out the enemy's intentions. These patrols seldom had much to report except a very dreary time in no-man's-land, shellholes filled with water and a desolate waste of ground that was almost impassable. Occasionally they met German patrols abroad on the same errand as themselves, but for the most part the enemy showed no activity.

These facts duly became the subject of intelligence-reports, and on the strength of them the higher commands decided that the morale of the enemy must be very low. They resolved to test that morale, probably with a view to exploiting further any success gained. All arrangements were made for a small local attack in the Brigade sector on the night of the 22nd of February, which should involve the capture of a section of German front by the 48th Battalion. Patrols had reported the presence of three formidable belts of wire entanglements in front of the enemy's trenches. In order to overcome these obstacles, the attacking party carried blankets which were to be thrown across the barbed wire. The attack was to have no artillery support, but was to be assisted by a barrage of Stokes mortars and Vickers machine-guns. Much reliance was also placed on the work which should be done by a party armed with rifle-grenades.

Such was the very inadequate means adopted as a result of the inadequate conception of the task on hand, an inadequacy that could be redeemed by no amount of attention to detail on the part of the unit concerned. The operation was attended by just such success as it merited. The first and second ridges of wire were successfully crossed, but the attacking party had a third and more formidable belt still in front of them. By that time the enemy who had been thought so dormant was very much awake. He sent up flares illuminating the whole area, whilst the ground was swept with his machine-gun fire. Fortunately the attacking party was a small one, and the broken nature of the ground enabled the men to take cover easily. They got back to their trenches having achieved nothing in an operation whose methods had no chance of success, and the Battalion congratulated itself on getting well out of an ugly situation at no greater cost than three minor casualties.

On the following night the 48th Battalion was relieved, and as was usual during a relief its patrols were in no-man's-land prudently guarding against a surprise attack. There a great surprise awaited them, for they could not discover any sign of the enemy immediately in front. Their curiosity led them to the opposite trenches, then right across the ground that had been the objective of the preceding night's attack. They returned and reported that they had failed to get into touch with the enemy, and that they thought he was withdrawing his forces. But the Battalion was even then being relieved, the further care of the front was in the hands of the relieving unit. Moreover scouts were not uncommonly credited with good imaginations. Nevertheless the scouts were in this case worthy of credence; for the enemy had begun that night the withdrawal which in the Spring of 1917 he carried east of Bapaume, falling back on the Hindenburg Line.

Chapter XI.

BULLECOURT.

WHEN the Battalion left the trenches on the night of the 24th, it began its journey back to the rest area.
Stopping at Mametz Camp for a few days, it continued the march through Albert to a wood near Henencourt on the 1st of March. The men showed all the signs of fatigue, for from the 7th of January till the 25th of February they had been continually in the front line or working immediately behind it. Winter in all the rigour of that winter of 1916-1917 still prevailed, and life in the huts in Henencourt Wood was dull and uninspiring.

The district around them, however, presented a very pleasant contrast to the scene of their recent labours They were in the midst of a peaceful, undulating country, that showed none of the havoc and ruin of war. Villages were near at hand and farm-houses were plentiful, where the men made many friends. Moreover, despite the unfavourable weather conditions, there was as much outdoor training as possible, which is perhaps the best antidote against the tedium of military life.

By this time the enemy had begun his retirement from that part of the line which the Battalion had last occupied. The middle of the month saw him leave Bapaume, and for a time it looked as if there was some chance of a war of movement having begun. So during the period of training at Henencourt, the Battalion practised attacks and following-up tactics in conjunction with the other units of the Brigade ;

and again speculation became active among officers and men as to the extent and importance of the operation in which they were next to take part.

Three weeks were thus spent at Henencourt before the Battalion again marched towards the east. Their first halt was at Fricourt, where they spent four days. From there they moved into dug-outs about a mile north-west of the old familiar Flers, at a place called Eaucourt-L'Abbaye. There was as yet no touch of spring or promise of it, rain fell almost constantly, and when the unit had got thus far east it was once more living the old life of discomfort and mud. Working-parties were strenuously busy on the many jobs that called for attention on the lines of communication. Moreover a projected operation was much discussed, and hard training for it was the order of the day.

On the 1st of April the Battalion moved about three miles further north to Biefvillers, a village lying somewhat to the left of Bapaume. Still the work went on, training alternating with fatigue-work until the men felt that impatience which Australian soldiers always showed during the days immediately preceding a big operation. It was not an impatience that had any of the affectation of the fire-eater about it. Indeed the soldier's impatience at such a time is wholly natural. For previous to an operation almost every hour of his day is taken up in training for it or working for it. He is living in the desert wilderness of the trenches. He has no newspapers, no distractions of any kind. The coming operation occupies his whole mental life, making him gloomy and silently dreading it, or making him a noisy enthusiast for it with a gambler's impatience for the issue.

The war of movement had ceased, indeed it had never begun, for the enemy had made his withdrawal leisurely enough. There had not as yet been adopted the great methods, greatly conceived, that should compel him to continue a war of movement. East of Bapaume ran his great reserve system of defence, which was known as the Hindenburg Line, and there his well-controlled retirement came to an end. As has already been stated, on the night the 48th Battalion left the front line trenches at Gueudecourt, the Battalion scouts had come in reporting their inability to find any trace of the enemy in the trenches opposite. The retirement had already begun as the unit wended its way to the rest area. Now the enemy was far east of Gueudecourt, far east of Bapaume. Bullecourt formed one of his new strongholds, and the Battalion had come back from the rest area to assist in the assault on this new line of defence.

After spending a week in the ruined village of Biefvillers, the unit set out for Noeruil on the 8th of the month. The distance was considerable and the march had to be made during dark. It was past 2 o'clock in the morning before the relief was completed, and the men were in the trenches from which the attack on the Hindenburg Line was to be launched. The Battalion scouts were busy immediately and under cover of the darkness patrolled the country in front. What they discovered was disconcerting enough, for three ridges of barbed wire each some eight yards in depth stretched before them. When these obstacles had been circumvented, they found fifty yards further on a still more formidable belt of wire entanglements which ran right to the enemy's parapet.

Our artillery was to play no very important part in this operation. In every operation before Bullecourt and since Bullecourt the artillery's role was a conspicuous one. It would begin its allotted task several days before the infantry came on the scene, doing counter-battery work whose success should make all the difference to the infantry afterwards. The artillery was accustomed to cut the barbed wire for the infantry man, to cover him in his advance, to protect him whilst he "dug in" after having gained his objective. But there was to be no great bombardment preceding this advance; there was to be no preliminary counter-battery work. The Army Commander was General Gough, and it was commonly understood that he was placing full reliance on the tanks which were to take part in the operation. It was considered that if the tanks could make an easy path over the wire entanglements, there should be no necessity for the operation to start with an intensive bombardment, and the surprise of the enemy should be all the greater for the absence of any preliminary artillery display.

But in the actual working out of that ill-starred operation in which the 4th Australian Division took part, there was little element of surprise and but little success in any attempt to take the enemy unawares. On the left flank of the 4th Division were English troops, and on the morning of the 10th all were in position for the attack which was to take place at 4.30 a.m. There was heavy snow on the ground where the men lay at the jumping-off position awaiting the hour. The hour came but the tanks were still waited for, and the minutes passed whilst the men shivered with cold in the snow. All the time they saw grow the daylight which should make their position an exposed and dangerous one. There they lay for an hour and at last the order was given to retire to the trenches. And what a retirement was that! Those men got up stiff and cold and cramped, damning the tanks, the stupidity of the higher command that backed the tanks. They returned to their own trenches just as does a crowd disperse after a football match, no pretence at taking cover, no care for an enemy. The digger was thoroughly "fed up," the digger of all ranks, officer and private, and he showed it by his careless contempt for friend and enemy alike. The enemy saw the casual withdrawal, which made him aware that an attack on his trenches had been intended, and was now for some reason abandoned. He immediately began to fire on the retiring soldiers, having them at quite close range; but they had the luck which attends the imprudent and reckless, and got back to their trenches with very few casualties.

The enemy was aware, however, that he had narrowly escaped a formidable surprise attack, and he began a heavy bombardment of the area. Major Ben Leane of the 48th Battalion was killed and four of other ranks, whilst seventeen of other ranks were wounded. Poor Ben Leane, sergeant on Gallipoli, rouseabout with the Camel Corps in Egypt, adjutant of the 48th at its formation, major and second-in-command at his death. A man with all the force of character of his truculent brother, but of a disposition gentle as a woman. In his loss the unit had already paid heavy toll to Bullecourt.

On the following morning the attack was again attempted, the same programme being followed out. Again the men were lying in position long before the hour of 4.30 a.m., and again long after that hour they waited in vain for the tanks. The approaching daylight, however, did not delay, so at 5 a.m. the 48th Battalion was forced to begin its advance. From 4.30 a.m. the artillery barrage on that part of the front had rested on the enemy trenches east of Bullecourt, to prevent the fire of the enemy whilst our troops should advance. But just now that protecting fire lifted, the artillery acting according to scheduled programme which presumed the effective co-operation of the tanks with the infantry.

The men were therefore forced to advance over the open ground with little help or protection from either tanks or artillery. In doing so they suffered many casualties. They carried mats to bridge the heavy ridges of wire, which either artillery should have cut or tanks rendered ineffective. The bridging of that wire further reduced their numbers before they finally reached the objective, which they did shortly after 6 o'clock.

The position of the 48th Battalion was now a very precarious one. Every effort was made to get in touch with the troops on the right flank but without success. The intervening gap was strongly held by the enemy, and constant bombing attacks were necessary to keep him from further inroads. The 46th Battalion had taken the first objective, and now lay in support of the 48th which had passed through it on to the second objective. On the left flank of the 48th there was no sign of the English troops, and it was considered then that they could not advance as the tanks had failed them. Thus was the 48th Battalion left with both flanks in the air.

Meanwhile the tanks were in different parts of the field experiencing different adventures. Colonel Leane had established his headquarters in the shelter of a railway embankment, and there an officer in charge of a tank reported for direction of his services. The Colonel asked him to go to the assistance of the left flank of his Battalion. The officer promptly sent the tank in that direction, but it returned before getting within effective range. On its way back it was struck by the fragments of a shell that landed near it, and although still workable was quickly abandoned by the crew. All the enemy shells falling in the area immediately concentrated on that tank, until it was set ablaze and Colonel Leane's headquarters soon became the unhealthiest part of the field. Another tank crashed into a field orderly-room where field signallers were at work, and the air became blue with the language of the disturbed diggers.

Such was the history of the tanks in that sector at Bullecourt, farcical but that they were the clumsy cause of so much tragedy. "Had the tanks shown more pluck and initiative I quite believe things would have been different." That was the official report on the operation. Perhaps it is true. But one remembers those unwieldy machines in operations eighteen months afterwards, when they were more plentiful, more developed, and when there was no conspicuous lack of pluck or initiative in their crews. And one remembers that they were even then so uncertain and often so ineffective, that the success of no operation was ever left to depend solely on them. At Bullecourt the fault seemed to exist in the criminal lack of foresight that entrusted the success or failure of that operation to an experiment with them.

But incidents of futile heroism were plentiful in the front line trench. Young Watson of the 48th had his brother killed beside him, and at the same time fell partially paralyzed across the brother's body. There he lay for two hours doing what work he could with his rifle, and then crawled back across the snow only to die two weeks later. The Germans advancing along the network of trenches were time after time bombed back. Bombs and more bombs were called for, and finally the 48th men began using the German bombs which were plentiful in that trench but lately vacated by the enemy. The German bombs are not so effective as ours, and the enemy argued shrewdly that ammunition must be scarce with this small garrison. So the first German bombs that fell among the enemy were a signal to him for a fresh and more hopeful sally, and he came on with a cheer.

Meanwhile the troops in support of the 48th had been forced to retire an hour previously, and their place was promptly taken by the enemy, who now surrounded the men of the 48th on all sides. The latter began therefore to fight their way back, until they reached that support-line which had been the first objective of the advance and was again held by the Germans. There they succeeded in driving out the enemy and for the time being establishing themselves.

The new position, however, on the whole front of attack was untenable, and the Australians saw they could do nothing but fall back to their original position in line with the English troops on their left flank. The Australian Brigade on the right of the 48th consequently began to retire. The position of the 48th was being rendered still more desperate by the fact that our artillery were dropping shells very close to their trench, probably in the belief that it was still held by the enemy. An hour later, therefore, the dwindling garrison began to fight back still further, a small party of officers and men covering the retirement. Captain Allan Leane and many others fell whilst so employed, a number were taken prisoner, whilst the remnant regained their original positions and spent the afternoon and night searching no-man's-land for their wounded comrades.

During the night of the 11th of April the sadly reduced Battalion went back to Bapaume. Its casualty-list for the operation made the gigantic total of fourteen officers and four hundred and twenty-one of other ranks.

None of those engaged in that glorious failure made any attempt to minimise the enormity of the disaster. It was the first time and indeed the only time that the Australians had lost a great number of prisoners to the enemy, but in this case the loss in prisoners for the Australian Division concerned was a very heavy one. At the time there was little doubt in the minds of the soldiers as to the causes of that disaster. The failure of the tanks to carry out their work, and the failure of the British to attack on the left of Bullecourt, were the causes commonly and bluntly stated.

As to the failure of the tanks there was a decided unanimity. The standing stakes and untouched wire entanglements were indisputable witnesses to the fact that they had never got near to the Hindenburg Line. General Robertson, the Brigade-commander, in his official comment to the Battalion wrote that " the failure of the tanks upset all calculations." General Holmes was then commanding the 4th Australian Division, and whilst congratulating the Brigade " on the success achieved in breaking the formidable Hindenburg Line," bluntly added, "notwithstanding the failure of the tanks from which so much was expected in the direction of preparing the way."

General Holmes touched the truth of the matter, for the great Hindenburg Line had been broken, it had been occupied for several hours. There could be no disputing the success achieved by the units concerned, though so far as it affected the general issue the success was but a grasping of Dead Sea fruit.

The Army Commander through General Birdwood " fully appreciated the splendid effort made this morning by the 4th Australian Division, which so nearly achieved a great and most important success." But indeed the 4th Division had actually achieved all that was possible for it. It had penetrated the Hindenburg Line and gained its objective. The holding on to that narrow front, however, unsupported and air-flanked on both sides as it was, could have no hope of permanency. Even with the help of the British, it would still have been a very narrow front, compared with that on which troops were accustomed to operate in later days, when success became a characteristic of our operations.

Chapter XII.

THE COLONEL.

THE life of a Battalion on active service approximates very closely to the domestic life of the family. Its nine hundred odd are dependent on the central authority of their unit. That central authority fathers and mothers them, looking after every detail of their lives, however personal. It praises them and rewards them with small favours if they are good ; and plays the heavy father with a stern lecture and sometimes with punishment, when its big hulking children have been behaving badly. When the unit goes into the line the same authority guides their footsteps on the way up, encourages and directs them whilst they are there. If any of them are wounded, if any of them are killed, the immediate relief of the wounded, the last duties towards the dead, are the zealous care of that authority which tries so hard to fill the place of parents.

The parallel between the life of the family and the family life of the unit could scarcely be exaggerated. Just as the education and chance in life of the civil family depends very much on the head of that family, so is it with this military family represented by the Battalion and whose head is the Battalion-commander. What manner of man he is determines to a great extent the character of the officers he has under him. On the officers of the Battalion depend the efficiency of the unit at work, and its happiness and contentment at rest.

Such being the grave importance of a Battalion-commander's position, it is a matter of interest to members of the

48th or to any interested in their story to recall what stamp of man was their commander. This sketch of the Battalion would fall very short of its aim and object, if it omitted a particular account of him whose personality gave to the unit which he formed and led, its distinctive character.

Raymond Lionel Leane was too truly an Australian to have any inclination for discovering a line of ancestry, or much respect for the man who had no better claim to respect than the possession of one. He used facetiously recount a hazy tradition of a forefather who lived in Ireland in strenuous days, and was there hanged for being a patriot or shot for not being a patriot. His descendant having a generous partiality for weak causes piously hoped it was a hanging matter. Ray Leane's father, however, walked in the ways of peace, being a non-conformist clergyman in South Australia. The end of the war found his mother still alive; of her it is sufficient to say that five of her sons served from the outbreak of war, attained high rank, and two of them fell in action.

The self-made man, especially when he knows himself as the admirable product of his own manufacture, is often an unamiable being. That Ray Leane should have escaped being the latter was very much to his credit, for in a great measure he was self-made and was aware of the fact. To the orthodox educational institutions which train and adapt men for careers he owed nothing, for they dealt not with him. To wealth he owed nothing, for he began modestly enough his pursuit of it in his early teens. What must indeed have been the strongest influence of his early years, was the atmosphere of puritan ethics and non-conformist theology in which those years were spent.

So strong was this influence that he was not satisfied with bending his own early life to it, but even set himself the task of persuading the world to the desirability and necessity of his creed and conduct. Indeed Australia went near to losing a good soldier in order to gain a very indifferent parson, that is if Leane could have been an indifferent man in any capacity. Then that phase passed. Young Leane began to devote himself more exclusively to business, and soon his passion for wholesale conversion found an outlet for its energies in the competition of the market. The crude ideals of other days still survived to form a rather unrelenting character, even after the system with which he identified them had ceased to have more than nominal adherence. But contact with the world and its influence on a disposition naturally simple and warm-hearted, had thawed the frost of an early puritanism.

Leane, the rather successful business-man, threw himself with great zeal into the soldiering of the Commonwealth Military Forces, and in due time received a commission. When the South African war broke out he endeavoured to enlist in one of the contingents, but was rejected on medical grounds. Yet the present war found Leane a man of thirty-five, fit to take upon himself its fatigues and duties immediately it broke out, and still unwearied by its trials and labours when after four and a half-years it came to an end.

Captain Leane left Australia with the first contingent. As a company-commander in the 11th Battalion, he came through all the hard training which the First Division experienced on the desert in Egypt. He landed with his Battalion on Gallipoli on the morning the Australians began their great adventure. During the months spent there, he took part in one strenuous incident after another. He conducted a second landing that went near to ending his career, when one morning he scrambled ashore with a small party of men and lay for several hours beneath the steep bank of Gaba Tepe. The exploit was doomed to failure, the landing was accomplished under a hurricane of fire from the Turks, and it was soon apparent that withdrawal was inevitable. With the help of Tom Brennan, a regimental medical officer who was Leane's trusty lieutenant in many stirring episodes, he succeeded in getting all his wounded to the boats. It was but one of several forlorn adventures he was destined to lead, and his skilful escape from its consequences got Leane a Military Cross and a name among the diggers of being a good leader in a tight corner.

He was wounded on Gallipoli, but his wound was slight and kept him only a short time from his military duties. He received his majority and was temporarily in command of his Battalion before it left the Peninsula, which it did a few weeks previous to the evacuation. Afterwards he was awarded the D.S.O. for his work on the same front.

When the Fourth and Fifth Divisions were formed at the beginning of 1916, Major Leane was appointed to the command of the 48th Battalion. He came to France with the unit in June of the same year, and was henceforth with it in all its varied fortunes. At Passchendaele he was very seriously wounded and this involved an absence of four months from his command. It was his only lengthy absence from the unit, for a marvellously strong constitution saved him from any illness; and his holidays were brief and always taken when the Battalion was at rest. Even this absence occurred during a time when the Battalion was enjoying its only spell from hard fighting, and he was again back at the head of his unit before the heavy work of 1918 had commenced.

For his part in the fighting at Passchendaele he received a bar to the D.S.O. Later on he received the C.M.G. whilst still in command of the 48th.

Colonel Leane continued to lead the Battalion until the end of May 1918, when he was promoted to the command of the Brigade with the rank of Brigadier-General. The 48th was a constituent unit of his Brigade. His connection with his old Battalion therefore was still a very close one, and continued so until the early months of 1919 when the unit was gradually disbanded.

Leane the man was a study, and such a one as to make adequate description of him difficult. For he seemed to have no sole and dominant characteristic, except the characteristic of displaying many characteristics dominantly. See him in his happy moods, no man was more happy. His men really loved him, and with good reason. He ever identified himself completely with their lives. When they enjoyed themselves he enjoyed himself with them. At their sports, their concerts, their rough-and-tumble "buck" dances, he was not only with them but of them ; gay and boyish as themselves, in fact a big boisterous digger.

See him in anger, and see anger ennobled by the bigness of it. A stern, hard man in the conception and performance of his personal duty, he had little sympathy with those who culpably fell short of his standard. In a critical moment at Pozières, when the battle was fast and furious, he could be seen going about cool and alert as if he were immune and himself controlled all the agencies attempting his destruction and that of his unit, directing here, encouraging there. One forgot his own fears in admiration of the man. Then meeting an officer ill suited to standing the awful strain on mind and nerve, and too plainly showing his collapse, the Colonel was immediately roused to homeric wrath ; like a gigantic storm-god tossing about in that sea of destruction, he threw his head towards the smoke-hidden sky and appealed to the high heavens to know "what he had done that God should inflict such a windy b——d on him for an officer." And one forgot his own fears in irrepressible laughter.

In his sympathy, when sympathy was called for, there was the tender feeling of a woman. He had suffered hard strokes at the hands of war. His brother, Colonel Allan Leane, was killed. Major Ben Leane and a nephew, Captain Allan Leane, fell at Bullecourt whilst serving with the Battalion. It is remembered how on that occasion he searched among the dead bodies for that of his brother ; how he carried in his arms the remains of poor Ben and set up a rude cross over the grave which he himself dug ; how he then continued to give himself entirely to the care of his unit in that trying engagement. Those tragic bereavements never hardened

"Such was the Colonel, a man who lived with men and they despised him not.'"

him, and he who truly and literally scorned death ever showed something approaching a parent's emotion at the death of his men.

And what of Leane the soldier, the officer, "the old man of the 48th," Leane "the big fellow" as his admiring diggers used to call him? Leane the soldier was just Leane the man, and therein perhaps lay the secret of his success. He was pre-eminently a judge of men. In his choice of those who served him and his allotment to them of different duties, the good judgment of Leane the commander suggested Leane the acute business-man, placing salesmen in the different departments of his commercial business with a view to getting the best out of them. Pozières had taught him that this war was a young man's war. In his subsequent selection of officers he rode the lesson to death. The kindergarten henceforth gathered around him was known as Leane's pups. The pups were well worthy of the big mastiff that led them.

He was master of his Battalion when it was in the rest area, and that statement contains more than a truism. No petty crisis that might be provoked in his big mischief-loving family, ever bluffed Leane. His officers and men gave him a loyalty almost religious in its intensity. It was founded on respect, however, and all under him knew he would not depart one hair's breadth from principle to gain it.

He could take care of his Battalion when it was in the line. Never did his unit occupy any front of which he did not know beforehand every hole and corner. He had a genius for the details of a situation, a prodigious and never-failing memory that made trouble for any officer under him who was not master of the minutest particulars of his own task.

His courage in the line was too much an accepted fact to impress those who knew him and served with him. He was not the kind of man to whom one ascribes heroics, reckless bravery or dare-devil-Dick methods. His judgment was too clear, his will too strong. His bravery seemed the most natural thing in the world, just as it should have seemed. A clear judgment told him that loss of his life was nothing to neglect of his duty towards those under him. A strong will enabled him to act according to that judgment. Doing his duty was natural to the man and he did it naturally. If risking his life was incidental to doing his duty, he did that naturally also and without any of the fuss of heroics.

But the officers and men saw therein true bravery. They saw the bravery of the strong and well-balanced mind, even when they understood not the qualities of character that were its foundation, they saw the unerring judgment exercised in the field, and the efficient leadership on which their success and their lives so much depended. What they saw inspired in them a loyalty and an affection that probably made Colonel Leane's hard years with the Battalion the happiest period of his life.

Such was the Colonel, a man who "lived with men and they despised him not."

CHAPTER XIII.

BRIGHTER DAYS.

ON the night of the 12th of April the 48th Battalion, which had been so greatly reduced in numbers by the attempt at Bullecourt on the preceding day, left Bapaume for Albert. A few days later it was again back at Henencourt Wood. This, however, proved an unhealthy place for a camp, so the men went into billets in the neighbouring village of Millencourt. The weather was now quite fine, and all were already enjoying a foretaste of the beauty of spring in France. When Anzac Day was celebrated on the 25th of the month, the men were showing but little signs of the fatigues and hardships of winter.

Those few weeks spent at Millencourt were the happiest yet enjoyed by the Battalion. The surrounding country was very pleasant and outdoor training in the fields was an enjoyable recreation rather than a toil. The first weeks of May saw the unit in the same place, and on the 12th the 4th Australian Division was inspected by General Birdwood. The different units of the Division had at this time got the reinforcements so badly needed after Bullecourt, they had had a considerable spell and time for regular training. Never perhaps did the Division present such a fine appearance. General Birdwood addressed the officers and men, reviewing the good work of the Division and mentioning particularly the work of the 48th Battalion at Pozières and more recently at Bullecourt.

Only one thing marred the joy of the day, and that was Birdwood's announcement that the Division was to leave the 1st Anzac Corps and for a time be attached to the 2nd Anzac Corps. This was felt very keenly, for the 4th Division had an old comradeship with the 1st, 2nd and 5th Australian Divisions, whilst the Divisions of the 2nd Anzac Corps were as yet strangers to it. Moreover the diggers were ever fastidious in the matter of Corps Commanders.

Nevertheless the 48th Battalion in common with the whole Division had to get ready for its journey to the north of France two days later. It moved to Aveluy, and entraining there on the morning of the 16th arrived at Bailleul the same evening.

It was already known that an operation on a large scale was intended, which should involve the capture of the Messines Ridge. Every available moment therefore was spent in special training, equipment was inspected, gas-helmets tested, and all the preparation preliminary to an attack was in progress. The Battalion moved nearer to the line to a place known as Dou-Dou Farm, and from there working parties went forward every night to unload ammunition at the many hidden ammunition dumps that were being formed over the area. At the end of the month an order was published that every unit taking part in the operation, should send back to a camp at the rear one-third of its personnel. This was to obviate the weakness of past methods, by which a Battalion lost so many of its officers and specially trained men as to be seriously handicapped in training reinforcements. The practice of forming and saving a nucleus was a prudent one. This was the first time, however, that the unit had experience of it, and it caused much disappointment to many who were keen to participate in an operation which promised to be extensive and successful.

Only on the 6th of June was it known that the great advance in which many Divisions were taking part was to be attempted on the following day, every precaution having been taken to make all details in connection with the operation a surprise to the enemy. The 48th Battalion was not to take part in the advance but was to remain in Brigade reserve, the 45th and 47th being the units of the Brigade directly employed. But the Battalion was not destined to be long disengaged, for on the evening of the 7th two companies were ordered up to reinforce the 45th and 47th Battalions. These Battalions had had a very strenuous time, and as yet the objective of the Brigade had not been secured at all points. Two hours afterwards the remaining two companies of the 48th went to the front line to perform the same duty of reinforcing the other Brigade units.

The four companies of the 48th were now in the line, and apparently they were to perform a big task in the advance in which, according to previous plan, they were to take no part. For the operation which had begun so well was in its final stages proving unsatisfactory enough. Indeed it was not until several days later that the Brigade frontage was completely secured, as progress had to be adapted to the pace of troops on other parts of the wide front who were meeting with varying success. When the officer in charge of the 48th troops had got to the front line on the night of the 7th, he was ordered to advance with two companies on the line determined as the final objective of the Brigade. This he did early on the morning of the 8th and succeeded in making secure the right wing of the Brigade objective. On the left wing of the Brigade front things were not so satisfactory, and a fresh attack made there was followed by a counter-attack of the enemy which practically left the position unchanged. But that part of the line taken by the 48th companies was consolidated by them, and securely held until they were relieved by troops of the 45th and 47th Battalions on the morning of the 10th.

The companies of the 48th were then withdrawn to the rear where they rested for the day. After re-organising they set out again for the front line the same evening and relieved the 45th Battalion. The situation was still very obscure, part of the Brigade objective being held by our troops whilst a trench and several strong-points on the same line were as securely held by the enemy. In these latter places everything was quiet during the day, but at night the enemy's activity was very evident. This fact suggested the supposition that they were occupied only during the night, and that their garrison retired to trenches further back before daylight. To act on such a supposition did in the circumstances involve a gamble, but the Battalion-commander decided to gamble and gambled successfully. On the morning of the 11th he sent a strong fighting patrol forward after dawn, and captured the trench and strong-points without resistance. At the same time two field-guns were captured and a large quantity of ammunition. This success was followed up by small local attacks during the day, and by the evening the front line was connected with the Brigade front on the left.

The Battalion had sustained but sixty-one casualties during five days severe fighting in an awkward position. One officer and nineteen of other ranks were killed, whilst three officers and thirty-six of other ranks had been wounded.

On the 12th the Battalion was relieved and marched back to the village of La Crèche. The weather was still beautiful and the men spent several pleasant days in the area. They were then taken still further back in 'buses, and finally on the 21st settled down near Doulieu. Here they were in the middle of a farming community who were rather prosperous, farm produce was plentiful, milk, and eggs and butter, and with those commodities the men supplemented their rations. It was also the strawberry season. In fact no place offered greater counter-attractions to the estaminets than did the district around Doulieu.

The 29th of June saw the Battalion leave Doulieu and march to Ploegsteert, where with the other units of the Brigade it remained in reserve. The area was very dirty,

and working parties were constantly employed on it during
the day. At times the shelling was severe and here it was
that Major Howden was killed. Every night the wood in
which the men were camped was shelled heavily, and although
the casualties were not many, no day passed without its toll
being exacted. They were the kind of casualties that Australians least relish, for they were sustained not in active warfare but whilst sitting back in a dirty area where one could
only passively trust to chance. The little cemetery was
gradually extending during those couple of weeks at Ploegsteert Wood. Just at this time General Holmes, commander
of the 4th Division, was killed in the same area. Everyone
felt very happy when the Battalion marched away from the
place in the middle of July.

The Battalion now returned to Doulieu and to the usual
routine of training and lectures, which was always resumed as
soon as the unit got back to the rest area.

Towards the end of the first week in August it again left
Doulieu, and marching north through Neuve Eglise and
through Dranoutre came to Kemmel, a distance of about
fourteen miles. On the following day it took over the front
line south-east of Wytschaete. There was indeed no front
line here, but the position was held by a series of strong-posts
manned by eight or ten men with one Lewis gun. Patrols
were constantly working during the night between these
strong-posts. The ground was very low and marshy and the
position was altogether a bad one to hold as the enemy
commanded a good view of its approaches. This made the
work of relieving and the different changes between the
companies a difficult and dangerous task. Nevertheless the
casualties during this term in the line were very few, the men
avoiding trouble by getting away to the flanks or pushing
out to no-man's land when their positions were being bombarded.

The Battalion remained in this area, being occupied in
the front line or in Brigade support until the last days of

August. It then marched westward to rest at Zuytpeene, the last stage of the journey being over sixteen miles long. This spell in the rest area lasted for three weeks.

Those weeks spent in the quiet villages and country districts of France might be considered to have been very dull. But anyone thinking so is unaware of the constant activity that prevails in a unit from which a high standard of efficiency is expected. It is interesting to note here a programme of lectures delivered during this period in the Battalion :—

July 23rd.—Discipline, Morale, Responsibility of Officers and Non-commissioned Officers for leadership.

July 24th.—Drill, importance of it as a means to an end. Ceremonial, its value. Guards and Sentries.

July 25th.—Sanitation, in trenches, in billets, in bivouac, on the march. Life in Billets.

July 26th.—Fire Discipline, description of targets, judging distance, fire control, fire combined with movement.

July 27th.—" Medical," care of feet, rendering of first aid, use of field dressing, evacuation of wounded.

July 30th.—" Intelligence," patrols, messages, reports.

July 31st.—" Administration," parade states, company officer's routine.

August 1st.—" Protection," whilst on the move and at rest.

August 2nd.—" Organization," the section, the platoon, the company.

August 3rd.—" The Spirit of the Battalion," its record as a fighting unit.

August 4th.—" Co-operation of all arms," the platoon as a self-contained fighting unit.

These lectures were delivered sometimes to all ranks, sometimes to officers and non-commissioned officers. Every day saw several hours spent in training in the fields or in route-marching on the roads, and yet time was always found for this amount of theoretical training. When the soldier was not at drill or lectures he was definitely at recreation.

BRIGHTER DAYS.   93

Work or play occupied almost every moment of his day, and in this manner was it made impossible for life to be ever very dull for him.

During those weeks of September the Battalion had an opportunity of getting reinforcements, and by the middle of the month it was actually over strength. Very seldom indeed had this been the case with it. The men were in great health and spirits, and rather looked forward to playing a part in an operation that was then projected. They set out for Steenvoorde in 'buses on the 21st of September and two days later were conveyed in the same manner to a camp on the way to Ypres. Thence they proceeded on foot to the forward area around Ypres, their passage being very slow as the roads were congested by an endless stream of guns and vehicles going up for the attack on the high ground that lay due west of the town.

That operation took place on the morning of the 26th, and none of the units of the 12th Brigade took part in the attack. But after the advance the Brigade relieved some of the units which had made the attack, and during this term in the front area the 48th Battalion lay in support to the Brigade at Polygon Wood. There its work was principally that of salvage. At the same time it buried many Australian and German dead lying over the area who had fallen in the recent engagement. The Battalion suffered a considerable number of casualties, for the enemy was apparently searching for guns in the area occupied by the troops, so he subjected it to very heavy shelling.

The 1st of October saw the Battalion released from this comparatively easy term of duty, when it went to Westhoek Ridge and took up a position in old trenches and dugouts. On the following day it marched to a camp further back, whence it was again conveyed to Steenvoorde in 'buses.

Already there were signs that the summer was at an end. Since the Battalion had come away from unlucky Bullecourt in the middle of April until its second sojourn at Steenvoorde during the first week of October, the weather had been almost uniformly fine. Throughout that same period there were other features than the beauty of the French summer to make it a happy one. For the Battalion had played a conspicuous part in the operation at Messines Ridge, an extensive one which was a definite departure from the finikin methods of previous warfare. Unfortunately the hopes which the troops entertained that it should mark a permanent departure from those methods, were not justified by following engagements. But the part which the Battalion played in the latter was withal a pleasant one, weather conditions were of the finest and casualties were comparatively few. Now, however, the summer was gone, and after spending a week at Steenvoorde, the men of the 48th were again heading for the trenches to find out if their good fortune had gone with it.

CHAPTER XIV.

PASSCHENDAELE RIDGE.

ON the 10th of October the Battalion marched away from Steenvoorde to Abeele, where it entrained for Ypres. There was a light but fairly constant fall of rain during the day; and it required little rain to reduce that battle-swept area to a condition of sloppy mud. Seen against the dull glowering sky of the October evening, ruined Ypres looked a dreary place. The same evening after 8 o'clock the Battalion set out for Westhoek Ridge, when it was sufficiently dark to make movement of troops prudent. There it settled down in trenches and such scant shelter as the place afforded.

Next day the operation-order was received, according to which a section of the enemy's defences between Zonnebeke and Passchendaele Ridge was to be attacked. The 47th and 48th Battalions were the units of the 12th Brigade involved. On the left of the Brigade front the 3rd Australian Division was to operate whilst the 13th Brigade was to be on the right flank.

The operation was to be an extensive one involving a great number of troops. Yet time for preparation was very short as the attack was to be launched on the morning of the 12th. At midnight the Battalion left Westhoek Ridge, and started on its long journey to the line from which the advance was to take place. The journey in the dark over country broken up by shell-holes filled with water, and deep enough to drown unwary wounded who might fall into them, recalled some of the worst memories of Pozières Ridge. Those of the

Battalion taking part in the attack altogether numbered six hundred and twenty-one, viz., twenty-one officers and six hundred of other ranks. They were to be at the jumping-off trench an hour before the attack was to be launched; but such were the delays and incidents of that winding trail in the darkness that they arrived only eight minutes before the appointed hour.

The troops were therefore just in position when the barrage fell that heralded the beginning of the attack. The railway from Ypres to Roulers ran through the country whose capture was the objective of the operation. On the railway embankment rested the extreme left company of the 48th Battalion and the left flank of the Brigade front. Three companies of the Battalion advanced on an even front, the fourth company following up in close support.

Shortly after the advance started the enemy's defensive barrage fell on our lines just behind the jumping-off trench, and was so prompt and so well placed as to show that he was on the alert. But his infantry showed little resistance. Two officers and two hundred of other ranks were quickly taken prisoner by our men, and his only show of activity consisted in very effective sniping and machine-gun fire from pill boxes.

When, however, the Battalion with the units operating on the right of it had advanced some distance, it was soon evident that all was not well with the troops on the left flank of the Brigade. There, on the other side of the railway line, the advance seemed to have been checked almost at its start. The left company of the 48th Battalion was therefore compelled to stop, and to swing back so as to form a protecting flank for the troops on its right. At the same time machine-guns and trench-mortars were directed from the 48th front against the enemy trenches that opposed the troops on the left flank. In this way those troops were enabled to push their advance further, and the connecting company of the 48th Battalion advanced accordingly.

"Seen against the dull glowering sky of the October evening, ruined Ypres looked a dreary place."

But it was soon evident that no further success would be achieved by the troops on the left of the railway line. The extreme left company of the 48th front therefore set about permanently adapting its line to the task of protecting the companies on its right. The result was not an effective protecting flank, and the enemy's rifle and machine-gun fire from the left continued to thin our ranks along the Brigade front.

Whilst things were in this state it was brought home to the advancing troops that they must dig in somewhere so as to obtain cover from the continuous sniping. A party of men, therefore, composed of both 47th and 48th Battalions, rushed forward some distance and established several outposts. Others followed suit, and by 8 o'clock in the morning the Brigade front was established after a fashion and the work of consolidating the position was begun.

The adventure, however, had little chance of success. It was the old story of a flank in the air which constituted an inviting target to the enemy from whatever position he chose to aim at it. In such a situation communication with headquarters of the Battalion could not be effectively and adequately maintained, for rifles and machine-guns registered many chances against a runner getting through with his message. The practice was resorted to of sending two runners carrying the same message, and both would be victims to the flying bullets before they had reached their goal. Early in the morning contact was made by aeroplane with our men in the advanced outposts ; but after that they saw no more of our planes, and had to settle down to await what might be in store for them.

At 3.30 in the afternoon the enemy put a heavy artillery barrage on the positions occupied by our troops. Half an hour later his infantry could be seen advancing for a frontal attack, about four hundred yards wide and apparently with perfect confidence. But our rifle and machine-gun fire dispersed the advancing Germans and warded off this attack.

H

Shortly afterwards his infantry again formed up, this time in even greater numbers but advancing more cautiously. It was soon manifest that our fire would not avail to stop this sally, and our men had to fall back from the outposts which they had established in front of the new line. The poor fellows in those outposts had a hard fate; for whilst withdrawing from the frontal attack of the enemy, they were cut down by the same murderous sniping from the left flank. Very few of them got back.

Meanwhile things were going no better at the Battalion headquarters, the mainspring of the Battalion's activities, which was a short distance to the rear. The 47th and 48th Battalions had their headquarters in the same place, at an old pill-box but recently evacuated by the enemy. When the enemy made his counter-attack at 4 p.m. the S.O.S. was promptly sent up by both Battalions. But the message brought no answering artillery, and the two Battalion commanders were engaged in repeating the signal when the enemy placed two shells on their headquarters in quick succession. It was fortune's last and hardest blow, for all around were gathered those details necessary to the work of a Battalion headquarters in the field—signallers, runners, stretcher-bearers, medical orderlies. Very many of them were killed and nearly all the others including both Colonel Leane and Colonel Imlay were severely wounded. Both units were thus deprived at the same time of most of the machinery necessary for their efficient working.

The German counter-attack was, however, for a time delayed in its development by the steady work of our Lewis guns. But the enemy now adopted different tactics, confining himself to a strong attack on our vulnerable left flank. By this time touch had been lost with the troops on that flank, and as a result of the new attack the 48th had to make a hurried withdrawal to a line further back.

It was then 5 o'clock in the evening and the hour brought no good fortune to the Battalion. For on falling back to this new line they still saw no sign of the troops on their left flank, and later discovered that they had retired to the original line. It was the last stroke and they made no further effort against such ill-fortune, but struck out immediately for the trenches they had left before daybreak.

Perhaps the hardest feature about the whole attempt was the fact that so many of the wounded were necessarily lost. When the Battalion retired, the enemy following up so closely gave no chance to any man who fell badly wounded. Indeed in no situation of which the writer has had experience, was such evacuation of the wounded as was possible attended with greater difficulties. For the journey of the stretcher-bearers was a matter not of yards, but of miles, over that marshy country where a wheeled vehicle was altogether impracticable. Eight men formed the ordinary complement necessary to carry a stretcher through the heavy mud, and many were the relays that had to be established on the route. Leaving the wounded behind, however involuntary and inevitable, is a bitter experience, and it formed a fitting and gloomy climax to the ill fortunes of the day.

The evening therefore saw our men back on the line from which they had started early in the morning. They had indeed captured some prisoners. They had inflicted considerable losses on the enemy when he counter-attacked. But their own losses were also considerable. Two officers were killed and one was missing, whilst eight other officers had been wounded. Among other ranks three hundred and fifty-nine were killed, missing or wounded, and this out of a total of six hundred and twenty-one officers and other ranks engaged in the operation. And they had gained not one yard of ground in return for the sacrifice.

Wherein lay the fault or what was the explanation of an attempt so futile and so barren of good results ? It could not easily be determined. But at the time prudent minds were very dubious regarding the outcome of an operation of which individual units concerned had such little warning, and into which they seemed to be so precipitously rushed. Rumour among troops is as impersonal as tradition. Like tradition also it is often deservedly laughed at, and like tradition it is sometimes very wise. Rumour had it that a highly-placed Australian General strongly but vainly protested to the higher commands that such artillery preparation had not been arranged as was necessary to warrant hope of success. His alleged protest seemed to be supported afterwards by the event. For it was the inadequacy of such artillery preparation that caused the attack to be held up on the extreme left, a hold-up that practically affected the whole front of attack.

The sadly reduced Battalion was withdrawn from the line and returned to Ypres under command of Major Brearley. Every article of equipment was deeply coated with mud. Rifles and Lewis guns were for the time being rendered useless from the same cause.

As our numbers were so small seven officers and one hundred and ten other ranks reported for duty from the nucleus camp, where they had been resting according to the order requiring a unit to leave a third of its effective strength out of the line. Thus reinforced the small Battalion went to Anzac Ridge on the 19th, there to remain in support. They were no sooner in position, however, than the Brigade was advised of other arrangements having been made. The 48th Battalion was relieved and marched away from the neighbourhood of Passchendaele.

CHAPTER XV.

THE BATTALION'S SPELL.

WHEN the 48th Battalion returned to the ruins of Ypres from Anzac Ridge it made but a short delay before continuing its journey to a camp in the reserve area. There at Halifax Camp it remained until the 26th of the month, when it went by train and 'bus through Wizernes to Cuhem.

The whole of the 4th Australian Division was now making its way back far behind the war zone. Everyone was confident that the Division was about to have the spell so long promised to it. Several of its units had lost very heavily in the recent fighting. It was therefore expedient that this particular time should be chosen for resting and to enable them to obtain reinforcements.

At the Village of Cuhem the Battalion remained for about three weeks and from there marched by easy stages towards the coast. The weather was then beautiful. The country through which the men marched was still showing the glories of a French autumn. The inhabitants had not before seen Australian soldiers. Indeed they had seen much less of any soldiers than had the war-worn people of the Somme. Their reception of the Australians was therefore an enthusiastic one in the different villages through which the men marched.

These circumstances made the march a very pleasant experience for the Battalion, and happy anticipation was at its highest when the village of Friancourt was reached. There the unit was to spend its term of rest.

This village was but a short distance from the coast. The smell of the sea was in the billets of the troops. The breakers could be sighted from their training-ground. Treport was near to them, and Eu, and other villages all within walking distance. In the country around them there was nothing except their own presence to suggest the existence of war. The sound of a gun was never heard, and an aeroplane, friendly or otherwise, was never seen. The district lay far away from the main roads of traffic, civil or military. The people of the district knew almost nothing concerning the war, and were indeed a much more kindly and pleasant people for that fact.

It was known as definitely as anything connected with a campaign can be known that the Battalion with other units of the Division should remain in this area until the middle of February. The last week of November was just begun when the 48th had settled down to its new billets at Friancourt. So the men were determined to make as comfortable as possible these billets in which they should have such a long spell and should spend the winter. The good French people gave them every assistance. Whilst the digger did a great deal for himself with the help of Madame, the Battalion used its powers of organization to add to his happiness. Football grounds were arranged and tournaments started. Concert parties were organised and many schemes were discussed for excursions to different places of interest along the coast.

This tranquillity, however, was rudely broken in upon when on the evening of the 3rd of December it was known through the Battalion that all ranks were to stand by ready to move at half an hour's notice. Many had gone away to the surrounding villages and returned late at night to hear that such orders had been issued. Later on it was known the unit should not move until the following day. Next day it transpired the enemy had broken through at Cambrai, but that it was even then uncertain if the 4th Australian Division should have to interrupt its rest.

The Division began to move from its present area immediately, after being there nine or ten days. On the night of the 5th the 48th Battalion left Friancourt at 11.30. The women-folk, young and old, of the village, shed tears at the departure of the Australians as if the stay of the latter had been a matter of years instead of days.

They marched that winter night to Eu, a distance of about four miles, and there entrained for Peronne. The journey to Peronne lay through the country made desolate by the first Somme offensive, and further devastated in the enemy's evacuation of it during the spring of 1917. The long train journey was not completed till late in the evening of the 6th. The Battalion then detrained at Peronne and marched to Hautallaines, a district some miles distant.

At this place the several Battalions of the Brigade were accommodated in one large camp. During most of the time here there was snow and frost, and the cold was intense in the wooden huts. It soon became apparent that the Division was not to be employed immediately in the front line, and that the stay of the Brigade in this camp might be a long one. So its several units settled down to make the best of the conditions.

General Robertson, having been granted a prolonged leave some weeks previously, the 12th Brigade was now commanded by General Gellibrand. The latter with the energy proverbially predicated of the new broom began training the Brigade as if it was a very raw and new formation. Brigade attacks were practised frequently, the Battalions skirmishing through the mud and charging over that desolate country until every rise and hollow on its surface was hatefully familiar to them. When these operations were not taking place the different units carried on their usual programme of training in their own grounds. But even then they were not free from the direction and criticism of the new Brigadier.

A strange man was Gellibrand, with the physique and bearing of a rather sickly University professor of mathematics, with hands stuck deep in the pockets of his breeches and the collar of his digger tunic hooked tight around his neck. He might be met in any part of his Brigade area. Nearly always on foot, he would casually lounge on to the parade-ground of a Battalion. After watching a young officer at work for some time he would begin such a quiet, lazy cross-examination as often to make the officer in question afterwards assert very emphatically that " the new Brig. knew too dam' much."

The energy with which he started remained with him, and during the weeks spent near Peronne the 48th Battalion along with the other units of the Brigade was kept very busy. Perhaps it was indeed a fortunate thing, not only for the efficiency but for the happiness of the men. For the camp was a bleak and desolate place, whilst Peronne was but a ruin and with its surroundings was destitute of all civilian population. The men were indeed accustomed to walk into Peronne of a night to attend a picture-show or a concert organized by the military, although the distance was some four miles and the season the middle of winter. There was but little attraction for anyone in the district, and life was perhaps made most tolerable by making it as active as possible on the parade ground.

Christmas Day was spent there, and despite the unfavourable circumstances it was a merry one and probably a noisier one than any Christmas the unit ever celebrated in France. New Year's day was made memorable by the fall of a German aeroplane in the 48th Battalion parade-ground.

The sound of a gun had not been heard for a considerable time except very faintly, and a hostile aeroplane had not been seen. When this machine was observed to be in difficulties, and then to descend so close to the camp, there was quite a sensation. Officers and men rushed to the spot. But the observer and pilot of the disabled machine were too quick for them, and had set fire to the aeroplane before they could be apprehended. This enraged the men, who were always keen on souvenirs from fallen planes, and but for some officers of the Battalion the Germans would have suffered rather rough treatment. The latter, who had descended easily and were unhurt, were made prisoners. The men of the 48th had to be content with telling lies to the other Battalions as to their share in bringing down the aeroplane.

A week later the Battalion left their camp at 10 o'clock at night, and marching to Peronne entrained there at midnight for the North. It was a cold and tedious journey and lasted until 3 o'clock of the following day, when the train reached Bailleul. Snow was falling heavily as the men detrained, and they immediately set out for billets, at which they arrived some three hours later.

The following day was the 10th of January, and that morning they were again on the march. They crossed the frontier into Belgium and took the train once more till they came to Elzenballe, a ruined village not far from Vierstraat, Ridge Wood and other places that were made familiar to them in the autumn of 1916.

That evening parties went forward from the Battalion to reconnoitre the sector to be occupied. On the following day the unit set out for the front line. It marched through Ridge Wood, past the old familiar brasserie, and then was carried on a light railway to a point on the Ypres-Comines Canal known as Spoil Bank. The strength of the Battalion was at this time about thirty officers and six hundred and twenty of other ranks. On the night of the 11th it was in the front line.

The position which the Battalion now held was not far from Hollebeke. Snow lay deep on the ground, but a light frost kept it dry under foot, and during this term in the line the conditions were quite pleasant. In the ten days that it occupied the front area the Battalion suffered but one casualty. The sector was very quiet, as at that season of the year there was little possibility of an attack being attempted by either side.

Yet there was every reason to fear that when weather conditions improved an attack would be made by the enemy. For the defence system in this particular place seemed incapable of defence, and promised success to any formidable assault made upon it. Moreover the outline of the country was particularly adapted to that pivotal method of sweeping attack on which Hindenburg was supposed to rely so strongly.

The line here had been held by one of those British Divisions that had been very much reduced in strength. Receiving no reinforcements they were employed on a sector where non-provocation of the enemy was the policy to be followed. This arrangement, sometimes necessary, had its advantages and disadvantages, and in this case the latter showed themselves in the state of neglect and disorganisation into which the defences had fallen. Immediately the Australian troops occupied this part of the front there began the proper organisation of its defence. Trenches had to be dug, strong-posts constructed and wire entanglements erected. The five Australian Divisions were in this northern sector at the time, and the same programme of reconstruction and preparation was being followed by all of them.

When therefore the 48th Battalion was relieved from the front line and went back to Curragh camp near La Clytte, it did not go back to absolute rest. Things were too busy in the forward area. Parties of men were daily being sent to Spoil Bank and beyond that point on road-making, laying cables, or some such work. The distance which these working parties had to travel from their Battalion was very great, and all ranks were glad when the unit once more set out for Spoil Bank in the middle of February.

It remained there until the middle of February, doing the same kind of work, but under happier conditions, for the men were nearer to the scene of their daily occupation. The Battalion then had to go to the front line again and during its week of duty there it had the same freedom from casualties as on the previous term.

On the night of the 20th February the Battalion was relieved and moved to a camp in the back area. There it remained until the end of the month, when it again crossed the frontier into France to spend a few weeks at the village of Meteren.

Colonel Leane had again joined the Battalion, from which he had been absent since wounded at Passchendaele on the 12th of October. Since that time the Battalion might be said to have enjoyed an unbroken spell. It certainly had no continuous spell from hard work, for whether in peace or war hard work is incidental to the life of any battalion that would maintain its efficiency. And during those months it had been enduring the rigours of winter. But those rigours were endured mostly in camp, it had had but two brief terms in the line, and that in a sector that was very peaceful. Its great spell, however, had been a spell from casualties in which the 48th had such a tragic record. Comparing these months with the full term of the unit's life, one may well refer to the immunity of this period as a spell.

Chapter XVI.

METEREN TO THE AMIENS ROAD.

METEREN is a small village in the north of France lying far apart from the great highway which runs through the Somme department, and is the main thoroughfare from Bapaume to Albert and to Amiens. Meteren and the Amiens Road are, however, inseparably connected in the minds of men of the 48th Battalion.

It was at Meteren that the Battalion settled down to the enjoyment of regular billets at the beginning of March 1918. Everything gave good promise of a very pleasant time. Bailleul, a town of considerable size, was but a couple of miles to the east of it. About the same distance away lay Merris, where the Battalion was billeted on its first coming to France nearly two years previously, and where old members of the unit had still many friends.

The weather was ideal, football matches were the order of the day and the absorbing topic of conversation. During that time the 48th was beaten at Australian football by the Australian Corps Headquarters, and some pointed remarks were made about people who were never near the firing line having plenty of time for practice. Equanimity was only restored when the 48th beat Corps Headquarters at Association football; but the 48th exponents were a few days later beaten by a team of Belgian soldiers and were henceforth regarded as having brought grave discredit on the Unit. The 48th beat the 47th at Australian football, and later on the 45th, but was beaten at Rugby by the 46th, as well as by the 12th Machine Gun Company. Great was the excitement of the debates on these matches and much "shrapnel" money changed hands on the results of them. On Sunday the 10th of March, after church-parade, a long day's sports began at which competition was very keen.

The long evenings had their own particular attractions. The regimental band, something very different from the fife-and-drum band of the days in Egypt, was a popular factor of entertainment, and the village boasted a cinema-hall where concerts were regularly organised.

During those days military training went on just as vigorously as did the round of games and entertainments. Rifle practice on the ranges was its principal feature. It is not difficult to introduce the element of sport into this form of training, so keen competition between companies and between platoons began to provoke nearly as much interest as did the football matches.

Life was very pleasant during the first half of March, and had reached that stage of happiness at which a Battalion usually proceeds to more strenuous things. In fact the 4th Division was just then expected to go forward for another term in the line. But a good holiday was being enjoyed and that anticipation cast no shadow over it.

Timid civilians began indeed to make troubled enquiries about this time of the officers, as to the probability of Meteren being involved in a fresh enemy advance, and as to the advisability of their leaving it whilst they had time to carry off some of their property. For the enemy had dropped messages from aeroplanes a few days previously, warning the civilians to leave Bailleul as he intended shelling it on a certain date. In this case the enemy was as good as his word for Bailleul was shelled at the time mentioned, and on the 21st of the month some shells fell around Meteren. Even that caused little anxiety, however, and next day there was a very merry gathering at the Brigade transport-show, where the battalions competed keenly for prizes, and the 48th was much elated with its success.

Meanwhile the rifle-range had provoked so much interest that a Divisional competition was projected. The Lewis-gunners of the Battalion wanted to share in the interest, and a range was allotted to them. On the morning of the 23rd the Lewis-gunners went to the range for a long day's practice. They broke off for the midday meal and got back to their quarters just as the companies returned from a route-march. Then it was that the Battalion received orders to be ready to move at an hour's notice.

When a large force is operating in the field, news filters through very slowly to the various units comprising it. Battalions, Brigades, even Divisions, are slow to get information concerning operations on another part of the front that do not immediately concern them. If their participation in them is required, orders are issued which necessarily involve some information, but usually only as much as is necessary for the performance of the immediate task. Therefore was it that the 48th Battalion had no knowledge of the great events that were just then taking place on the Somme, and knew not that the enemy was undoing during the last two days all the work that had been done since July 1916. Its members could but guess at the new destination of the Battalion so suddenly determined on; but readily presumed it could not lie towards that part of the front from which the enemy threw his few ineffective shells at Meteren, on the very day he began his work of undoing in the Somme.

The Lewis-gunners did not return to the range, all parades were cancelled, and all leave was stopped. During the afternoon the bustle of preparation for departure went on, rolls were called frequently, ammunition was inspected and checked. The cinema-hall ceased to entertain and was used to store the surplus stuff of the Battalion, the officers' kits and all the holiday gear of a unit's term in the back area. The old Australian flag which the Battalion used to carry was placed there, as well as some surplus band instruments.

When all preparations had been made, it was announced that the Battalion should not move until next day.

On the following day the Battalion's transport set out towards the south, for in that direction lay the great trouble and already the rumour had spread that Bullecourt was again in the hands of the enemy. The Battalion had to make a faster journey, and was to be conveyed by motor lorries. But it was not until Monday morning the 25th that it was finally carried away from Meteren. A few men were left behind to guard the stores in the cinema-hall, the old Australian flag, the kits and the band instruments. Nothing was heard of those stores again, for not many days afterwards Meteren and its cinema-hall were in ruins.

The effective strength of the Battalion at this time was thirty-eight officers and six hundred and eighty-six of other ranks. The long line of lorries required to accommodate that number, was but one of many hurrying with Australian units in the same direction. Definite routes allotted to each column had to be strictly adhered to, if congestion was to be avoided. Good and familiar roads could not always be chosen, and in that precipitate journey the bye-ways met were many and intricate. It was evening when the Battalion arrived at Beaumetz, a village about six miles southwest of Arras.

At this point the officer in charge of the motor-column protested he could go no further, so the remaining four miles of the journey to Berles-au-Bois were made on foot. Arrived there the Battalion found orders awaiting it to patrol the roads, and to select battle positions which were to be manned immediately the alarm was given.

Next day was a day of rumours so conflicting that no one knew what to believe. The men were never in more humorous mood, for the excitement and uncertainty was great. Many protested their willingness to swear that no enemy had broken through at all, but that certain people had "simply got the wind up." Colour was lent to this view of the matter, by a report received from a neighbouring Corps to the effect that German armoured cars were making towards them. The rollicking diggers rolled out to man the cross-roads, only to find that some French traction-engines were the cause of the alarm.

In the evening orders were received to take up a position about two miles south of Berles-au-Bois, and bivouac there for the night preparatory to moving into the line. About 7 o'clock the unit started for the place, the 45th and 47th Battalions having already gone on ahead. The latter were just then seen to be returning and it transpired that the orders had been cancelled. Some time later fresh orders were issued requiring them to march immediately to Senlis.

Senlis was some 12 miles nearly due south of Berles-au-Bois, and at 10 o'clock at night they set out on their long journey after a rather anxious day. The route lay across the battle-front that was ever coming westward, and when or at what point the enemy might be met no man knew. To guard against such uncertainty small patrols marched some 2000 yards on the left flank of the column, whilst a platoon was detailed to guard the transport which had by this time rejoined them. It was a beautiful clear moonlight night and a big body of men would have presented a good target, whilst the continual rat-tat of the machine-guns left no doubt as to the enemy's proximity.

On through Bienvillers they marched, through Souastre, through Coigneux, through Betrancourt. Once they halted for an hour, and immediately almost every man in the column was asleep by the roadside. Then on again through Force-ville, through Hedauville, and as they approached Senlis in the early morning of the 27th, German shells were passing westward over their heads.

At Senlis they found small parties belonging to various English units, but the men were too tired to fraternise or to be curious for information. They had breakfast, a brief spell, and at 10 a.m. they moved again, going through Henen-court and on to Millencourt. There in a hollow behind the old cemetery, on the western side of the village, they sought such shelter as was obtainable from the shells that were falling in the area.

It was here that an English staff officer approached the unit to tell a breathless tale : Dernancourt had been taken by the enemy ; the Germans now held the railway-line in front of Albert ; they were still advancing ; he had been sent to guide the Battalion into position immediately. The Battalion commander asked him for his authority. He had none in writing ; he had seen the Brigadier of the 12th Brigade ; by the latter he was sent with these instructions. What was the Brigadier's name ? He had heard it but he really could not remember. And Colonel Leane fixed him with his murderous stare. This completed the demoralisation of the poor fellow. Asked by the Colonel in what direction he proposed to guide the unit, in his embarrassment he indicated a direction that confirmed suspicion regarding him though his utter confusion was an easy explanation of the mistake. The circumstances indeed could not be lightly accepted in that uncertain and anxious moment. The Colonel refused to follow the instructions ; the officer was retained as a spy. The Brigadier was communicated with, and the result exonerated the staff-officer. He went away with a very bad impression of Australian respect for the staff.

The Battalion immediately moved forward. It was about the middle of the day, the weather was very fine, giving good visibility to the enemy whose observation-balloons could see the advancing troops and soon brought heavy artillery-fire to bear on them. The black " woolly-bear " shrapnel, on which the enemy so much relied for demoralising troops, burst over their heads, whilst our own artillery blazed away behind them. The men were well spread out in artillery formation, however, and with the 47th Battalion on their right, got to their position without any casualties.

This position was some two thousand yards behind the railway line on the right side of the road. Matters were not so bad as the staff-officer reported. Troops of two Scottish units held the railway embankment on the right side of the road, whilst that on the left side was held by the enemy. English troops had there swung back to a line which they still occupied.

Throughout the afternoon the 48th lay in support of this line. The enemy's guns were active, but no casualties were experienced except from a British low-flying plane, whose pilot directed machine-gun fire on the trenches thinking they were occupied by Germans. In this way one man was killed and four wounded, the subsequent explanation being that air-men were instructed to fire on all troops east of a certain point. The instruction involved an enlightening comment on many events of those first trying days.

On that evening one very auspicious change took place. General Rawlinson, in whose Army the Australian Divisions were henceforth to achieve an unbroken series of successes, had been hurried back from Versailles. The possibility of continued enemy advance extending even beyond Amiens, required the construction of important reserve defences on a large scale. General Gough and his staff were released for its direction and supervision. This necessitated the appointment of General Rawlinson to the command of the British forces south of the Somme ; so the Australian Corps that evening began a new career in the Fourth British Army.

During the night the Battalion moved up to the railway embankment on the right of the road, and relieved the Scottish troops who were holding it. The unit had left Meteren only two days previously, but had experienced a weary time before it finally began its task of barring further progress along the Amiens Road.

CHAPTER XVII.

THE DEFENCE OF AMIENS.

THE task which the 48th Battalion now found itself called on to perform, resembled more that of a fighting patrol on a large scale than of a unit appointed to relieve another definite unit holding a definite line. For more than one unit was represented in the small body of troops relieved; whilst the particular line of defence which they occupied seemed not the result of any deliberate choice, but rather to have been adopted haphazard on the ground that it was as good as any other position. That morning the same troops had held the left bank of the river Ancre, nearly one thousand yards further east. The oncoming enemy gave them little time to seek the best advantage in choosing a new position, and the railway embankment, which was very high for the greater part of the way, seemed at first sight favourable ground from which to block or retard further advance. Of the enemy's whereabouts nothing was known, and the relieving Battalion's first duty was to discover those whereabouts and the points from which fresh attacks were to be expected.

Scouts were immediately sent forward who crossed a road which ran almost parallel with the railway line. They proceeded a considerable distance without encountering any of the enemy. Other patrols went towards the left flank of the Battalion front, and finally got into touch with English troops. The left flank of the 48th swung back from the railway line at a point about two hundred yards south of the Amiens Road, and linked up with the English. Only two companies of the Battalion were in the front line, and were holding about thirteen hundred yards of front. The remaining companies were in close support. Thus finally adjusted they settled down to await further happenings.

Nothing of much importance happened during the night. The enemy was holding the railway line on the left of the Battalion flank, and there had a machine-gun position established on a railway bridge. In front of the right wing of the Battalion another machine-gun from the protection of a saw-mill kept up a sweeping fire on the line. Except from these two points, however, there was little sign of enemy activity during the night. The district had recently been a quiet, peaceful place to which the refugees of 1916 had long since returned, and had again got together the makings of settled homes. Frightened hens made a homely noise in no-man's-land, and calves could be heard moaning plaintively as they wandered about in the darkness. One neat little home stood near the embankment, where some scouts found fresh-laid eggs and also secured a few fowls. It was neatly furnished and they spent the night there, and suffered no harm though its windows were smashed by machine-gun bullets. Next day the enemy used heavier material against it and the pretty home was soon an unsightly ruin.

In the morning a heavy fog obscured everything, but shortly after 5 o'clock began the first of a series of strange incidents. German soldiers carrying full packs and in most cases with their rifles slung over their shoulders, were seen coming through the fog across no-man's-land. All along the front from the south side of the railway and away to the right flank of the Battalion they came on, great figures advancing confidently in quite close formation. Nothing more than the desultory artillery-fire that had been kept up during the night accompanied their advance. There was no preceding barrage to give warning of their approach. They did not attack, they simply advanced. Never before in the course of the war had Australian soldiers seemed to be treated with contempt by the enemy, and the diggers felt honestly puzzled as they swept the oncoming Germans with rifle and machine-gun. On the right flank of the Battalion some thirty of the enemy actually got through the outposts of the neighbouring unit. They surprised two men whom they made prisoners and casually continued their onward march. The right company of the 48th saw what had happened, and an officer and party of men swinging round soon made prisoners of both captors and captives.

Those thirty German prisoners were well examined before they got back to the rear. The digger ever evinced a most intelligent curiosity regarding what might be called the Fritz mentality. He was not only interested to know what the Germans had thought of certain engagements, of the fighting qualities of certain troops, whether the enemy had a proper fear of Australian troops. He was also anxious to have explained certain German cruelties of which he had heard, to probe the enemy on the treatment he was supposed to mete out to our snipers he might capture or to our wounded. The Fritz often spoke English, and the digger spoke with frank curiosity concerning a mental and moral waywardness which he could not understand. He did so with no gratuitous intolerance, for the soldier of the fighting unit had little " Hun-hate," contemning that as the characteristic of the button-day patriot at home or the people in safe jobs abroad. He certainly " souvenired" his prisoners thoroughly and was little concerned about the etiquette or the ethics of the practice. But when he had taken a prisoner's watch, and pen-knife, and his buttons or badges, he would hand back with honest reverence a mother's photo, and present the robbed one with some biscuits and a cigarette. Then immediately the questions began, questions so obviously asked for the intellectual satisfaction of the questioner rather than in the hope of getting information of military value, that the digger probably succeeded in getting far more interesting material than the people of the Intelligence Service.

On this occasion curiosity was at a high pitch for an explanation of the strange method of attack, and the explanation forthcoming was indeed strange. Asked what their objective was the answer came that they had no objective. They were simply to march towards Amiens, when they were tired other troops following on motor lorries should take their place and continue the march. They themselves had been brought to the vicinity of Albert on the preceding night by motor lorries, they had a drink of coffee in Albert at 3 o'clock that morning and at 5 o'clock started on their forward march. Yes, it was at Albert that they got the English cigarettes and the socks with the Australian Comfort Fund mark on them. This gave rise to some angry discussion among the diggers as to why their socks should be kept in Albert when the Australians were fighting in the north. But a chance remark by a German prisoner that he thought the Australian Divisions were in the north of France diverted their short-lived anger. With much laughter they assured him that he and his comrades had "come a gutzer," "had slipped a kilo." Then they rescued the Australian socks from the German packs and impounded the English cigarettes, and solemnly told the prisoners to go back to the rear and consider themselves very lucky men.

Again the enemy advanced and again rifle and machine-gun took their toll of his ranks, and sent them scurrying back to the wood and to any cover afforded by the buildings that lay on the outskirts of Albert. Nine times during the day did he thus attempt to advance. Each time his approach became more cautious, and each time he received better support from his trench-mortars and machine-guns. But he had little chance of success with the tactics he was adopting. The Ancre, which ran in front of the railway line, had been spanned by narrow foot-bridges. Across these his soldiers had to file and then assemble in the wood to renew the attempt. From an observation-post in rear of our front line this assembling could be easily seen. The infantry communicated the location to the Australian artillery that was supporting them, and the 18-pounders swept the road on the right bank of the Ancre where the Germans were congested whilst waiting till those in advance had slowly filed across the foot-bridge. The Germans who got across found their assembly-point in the wood raked by the same murderous fire.

The Battalion was now thoroughly alive to the situation, and no movement of the enemy escaped the observers stationed at different posts. Artillery and infantry were working in perfect liaison, the latter finding targets for the former who promptly brought their heavy fire to bear on them whilst the infantry finished the work with their lighter weapons. Thus about two hundred of the enemy rushed forward into buildings on the left flank of the Battalion front. It was a most vulnerable part. The railway line was low there and already in the hands of the enemy. It would have required but another quick sally to outflank the Battalion on that wing. But again the artillery was requisitioned, and as the Germans hurriedly evacuated the buildings our rifles and machine-guns had them at close range. By evening things were fairly quiet. Further attempt at advance seemed to have ceased, and the ever-watchful observers saw great congestion of transport retiring in the direction of Pozières on the main road from Albert. Apparently the enemy had decided to change his tactics, but little opportunity of escape was given him. The heavy artillery were communicated with, and soon the observers could see the horses of the enemy's transport galloping frantically across the open country.

That night passed quietly, and during the next two days the Battalion was little troubled by the enemy except for one abortive attack on its vulnerable left post. But the enemy's machine-guns forward of the right and left wings of the Battalion front were as active as ever. His shelling was not too severe but his trench-mortars were gradually adding to our list of casualties. Nevertheless, but two companies held the 48th Battalion front. More than one relief took place between them and the other two companies in immediate support, for it was a trying vigil. The troops, however, were never reinforced although their numbers were gradually diminishing. Twice a Lewis gun and its team were blown out by shell-fire, and two new guns went forward with fresh teams from the supporting companies. That was all. The 48th had long ago learnt its lesson against the tactics of congestion that cost lives, and since that time had systematically and successfully gambled with many a situation.

The position being held was a peculiar one. Immediately south and to the rear of the Battalion lay Dernancourt, securely held by the enemy whose line ran still further west of that village. Again to the north our line swung back so that the unit's front formed a petty salient. The position would probably never have been held but that, as has already been indicated, the 48th went into action rather as a strong fighting patrol looking for the enemy and with little information as to his whereabouts. The war of movement that was to be so applauded a few months afterwards, was already being enacted in a most thorough manner. In this case, however, the enemy was dictating its character. It was that war of movement which enabled the position to be held so long as it was held. It was already anticipated by those on the spot, that when the war in that part should have become sufficiently stationary to allow of the enemy making a proper appraisement of the situation, the consequent revision of tactics might cause a sudden end to the salient. Meanwhile the 48th was determined to lose as few lives on it as possible. So on the night of the 30th of March when it left the trenches for a spell its casualties during the three days bore a happy comparison with the strenuous work performed. On the first day two officers and eleven of other ranks had been killed, whilst one officer and forty-five of other ranks were

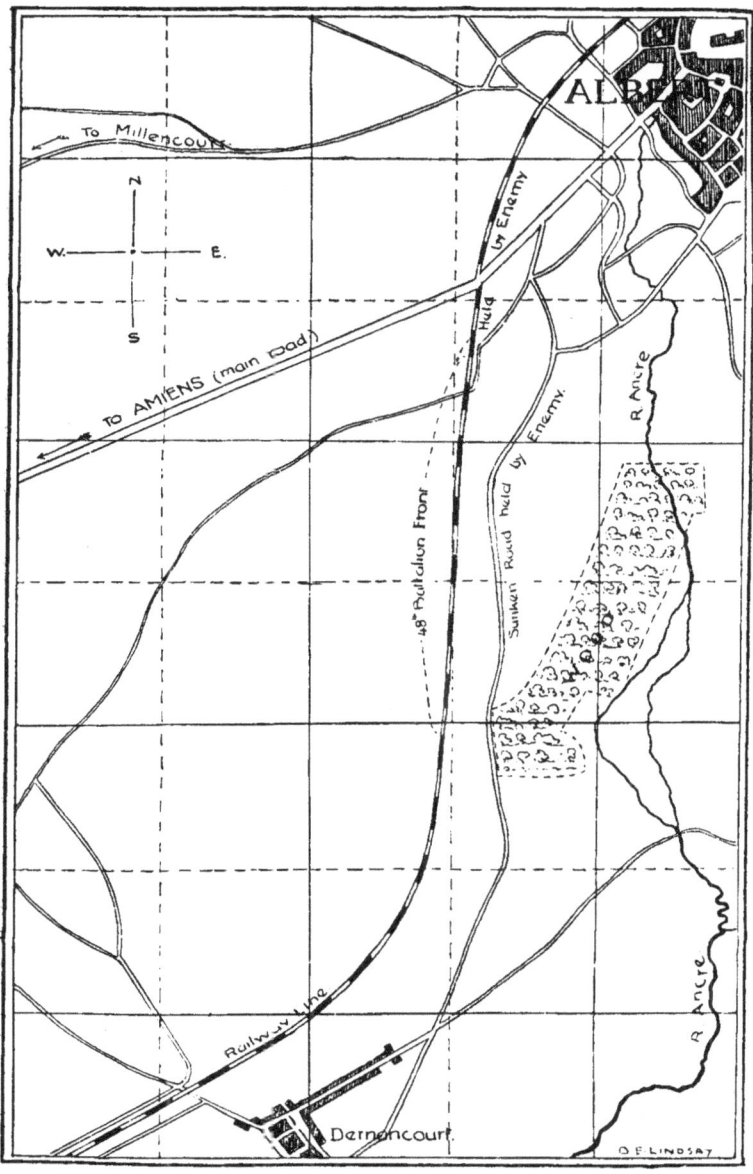

Map showing the Battalion's Defence of the Amiens Road (drawn to scale).

wounded. On the following two days there were no fatal casualties, but twenty-one of other ranks were wounded.

The Battalion moved back to Millencourt some two miles to the rear, where it was subjected to heavy shelling from the enemy and several casualties were inflicted. It remained there for three days and on the evening of the 3rd of April again set out for the railway embankment. The unit was in its old position about 11 o'clock. This time it had extended its front on the left to the Amiens Road, and there established a formidable strong-post. In this part of the front the enemy could approach more easily under cover of trees and buildings, and his anxiety to clear a passage along the main highway was very evident. So the necessity of securing the defence of this vulnerable part as well as the extension of frontage, required the employment of three companies in the line with one company in support.

On the following day the enemy's shells were travelling continuously over the men's heads away to the back area. The enemy was evidently searching for our heavy-gun positions. Then his range shortened and he began systematically searching for the light batteries. He had plenty of artillery, his own artillery reinforced by good English guns and English ammunition captured in the recent advance.

What has been written of the German adherence to programme in military tactics is not all of it fiction. Those who held the line against him and whose lives so often depended on what they could guess of his future movements, had usually very accurate premonitions. All felt that something great was intended, and this became conviction when the enemy began to register all along their front with trench mortars. During the night scouts went forward cautiously to see if more could be learned. A road which ran some two hundred yards in front of our lines was found to be held by the enemy, whilst preparation seemed to be in hand for a fresh attack.

Nothing happened until about 6 o'clock on the following morning, when some fifty of the enemy advanced towards the left post of the Battalion and were easily driven off. An hour later he concentrated the heaviest artillery fire on the Battalion support and reserve area. The bombardment was intense, the heaviest that the unit had suffered since its experience at Pozières nearly two years previously. Then about 8 o'clock his barrage fell on the front line where his artillery and trench-mortars began to do great damage. Gas-shells were numerous, and the men had to don their gas-helmets and peer through the dim glasses to watch for the enemy's coming. More than an hour had elapsed before he appeared, and then he was seen to be advancing in large numbers. The 48th clung to the railway embankment and after stiff fighting the Germans were driven back. That portion of the railway line immediately south of the Amiens Road was already held by a strong enemy post, and in this already vulnerable corner he endeavoured to develop his advantage. His troops pushed over the railroad at this place, and advanced in great numbers through a ravine towards that part of the Battalion's front which swung from the railway back to the main road.

In the little corner formed by the railroad and the highway to Amiens, there now ensued a short period of strange warfare. It was for the time being cut off from the rest of the battle and both contending parties were free to fight undisturbed for mastery. Time after time the enemy attacked towards the opposing line and was driven back by rifle and machine-gun fire to such cover as the ground afforded, only to reorganise for a fresh attempt. Then individual bravery began to show itself in the assailants. One of them rushed forward with their heavy type of machine-gun, but was shot down before he had proceeded far with his burden. His place was readily taken by another who soon met the same fate. Yet a third German picked up the gun and was essaying the task with some chances of success as the Australians admired him and shot him. After that the Germans dug themselves into a bank and the sniping began. Where a head showed itself on either side a shot immediately rang out. The enemy suffered heavily in this position being constantly subject to cross-fire, and for the time being had no chance of making further headway.

One incident occurred about this time that was the subject of much amusement afterwards. The 48th Battalion and the Germans holding positions on the same railway line, that part which lay between the enemy's extreme post on the railroad and ours constituted a kind of lateral no-man's-land. This narrow strip of territory was a hunting-ground for snipers of both sides, who used to steal cautiously by the side of the railway embankment and under cover of the trees. One 48th sniper was thus making his way towards the enemy when he saw a German soldier not far from him advancing in his direction and evidently bent on the same errand. Recognition was mutual and simultaneous, and each being at that moment near a friendly telegraph-pole darted towards it and stiffened himself against it. Then the Australian whipped round and had a quick shot ; the German was equally quick, but both shots missed. Immediately they again tried to adapt themselves to the diameter of the inadequate poles. The operation was repeated and two shots again rang out and once more inflicted no harm. That was enough, and Fritz and digger each ran headlong for his own lines and his own life.

The enemy compelled a withdrawal of the line on the remote right of the Battalion front. At that part the line had already swung back considerably, and it required but a slight retirement to make untenable the position of the unit on the right of the 48th. That unit now retired, with the result that the Battalion's right flank was in the air. For another hour the 48th Battalion held on to its position on the railway embankment, whilst subject to fire from its rear where the enemy had already made some prisoners.

The situation required careful handling to prevent the two companies holding the railway embankment from being cut off. It was here that Captain Cumming's ability so conspicuously displayed itself. He was in command of that company which for the time being had adjusted its own quarrel satisfactorily on the extreme left of the Battalion front. An officer who loved a puzzling situation for its own sake, this one gave him the novel experience of being able to protect both flanks of the retreating companies. Whilst part of his men engaged the enemy threatening the left flank, others kept up a continuous machine-gun barrage on Germans attempting to approach the right flank from Dernancourt. In this way the two companies were safely withdrawn some twelve hundred yards back, where they established a line of outposts running north and south of the Amiens road and also took up a position in a well-dug trench further to the rear.

In the angle formed by the railway line and the main road, Captain Cumming's company still remained. Its ranks had already been thinned by casualties, and the enemy now further threatened it by occupying immediately the positions evacuated on the right. Its retirement was ordered, but before this could be accomplished the troops on the left, north of the road, had to be apprised of the situation. Efforts to communicate with them by visual signalling failed, and young Tregoweth, a signaller, undertook to run the gauntlet across the Amiens Road with a message. He fell badly wounded when about one hundred yards from a post on the other side of the road, and after he had crawled for some distance men were seen to rush out and carry him to safety. Apparently he was able to deliver some part of his message, for the unit holding that part of the front immediately signalled asking for information. It was made acquainted with the position on the right and forthwith retired to the new line further back, whilst all that was left of Cumming's company withdrew in line with the remainder

" . . . . Captain Cumming . . . . an officer who loved a puzzling situation for its own sake, ..."

of the Battalion after enduring three hours of splendid isolation.

The Battalion's front now extended right across the Amiens Road north and south of it. The diminutive salient had ceased to exist and nobody regretted it. The new line ran over high ground which commanded a good field of fire in front. During the night and on the following day the enemy gave little trouble, and on the night of the 6th the Battalion was relieved by other Australian troops and marched back to trenches north of Bresle. Next day it went to Bussy-les-Daours, about eight miles further to the rear.

The unit's casualties during the fighting from the end of March till the morning of the 7th of April showed a total of three officers and thirty of other ranks killed; three officers and one hundred and eighteen of other ranks were wounded, whilst forty of other ranks were missing. When regard is had to the character of the fighting and to the daily average of a unit's casualties even when holding a quiet front, this total does not seem so formidable. The Battalion had played its part well in a great work.

Chapter XVIII.

MONUMENT WOOD.

MANY were the changes of plan and destination for the Battalion in those days of uncertainty. On the 9th of April the unit set out for Coisy, a village some six miles north-east of Bussy-les-Daours. After spending a day there it again packed up its many belongings, its pots and its dixies, its boilers and water-carriers, and trudged off just the same distance north-east of Coisy. The Battalion having thus solemnly marched the two sides of an equilateral triangle settled down at Beaucourt on the 12th of April, and used bad language about people who sat in high and comfortable places unable to make up their minds.

Very urgent work was apparently required of the Battalion. On the following day all hands were busy on the construction of strong-points that were to form part of a reserve line of defence. The men worked all through the night and till 6 o'clock on the evening of the following day. Afterwards the unit carried on the work in two shifts, the first from 7 a.m. till 1 p.m., and the second from 1 p.m. till 7 p.m. When the strong-points were completed, the work of linking them up was begun, and on the 18th of the month that portion of the reserve line allotted to the Battalion had been completed.

On the same date General Gellibrand was invalided and Colonel Leane took charge of the Brigade. Major Allen temporarily assumed command of the 48th. Under these changed circumstances the unit settled down to training its reinforcements ; whilst every day officers went forward to reconnoitre different parts of the front line, that they might be prepared in case the Battalion was ordered into action at short notice.

The men were looking forward to spending an unusually dull Anzac Day at Beaucourt. On the morning of the 23rd, however, they heard the enemy's heavy gun-fire, and it became only too plain to them that he was attacking some part of the line. It was soon evident that Anzac Day should not be spent at Beaucourt, and at noon of the day preceding it orders were received for the Battalion to be ready to move at an hour's notice. It did not actually leave Beaucourt until late in the evening, and then went no further than Pont Noyelles, a village lying some three miles to the south. There the night was spent, and when Anzac Day dawned it gave every promise of being exciting enough even if not very festive. Motor 'buses soon arrived showing that the next destination of the Battalion was to be some distance away, and that no time was to be wasted in marching. All surplus kit, packs and blankets were dumped, and the unit stood ready to embuss at fifteen minutes' notice.

Nothing definite was known by anyone of the Battalion as to the reason for all this despatch, but it was generally understood that British troops had been pushed out of Villers-Bretonneux. All waited, but still no word came to embuss. Then someone remembered that it was Anzac Day, that the members of the regimental band were not required to go into the line, that therefore the band should be doing something to earn its rations. The poor band, many were the times that it was reminded of its immunity from the risks and fatigues of the line ! The band therefore turned out and gave an excellent concert which lasted for nearly three hours. By this time night had fallen and the 'buses still remained unused. The report then began to spread that Australan units had restored the broken line, and such a thing being very probable, and in the circumstances very desirable, the 48th casually accepted the rumour and went to bed. It afterwards transpired that on the morning of the 23rd the enemy had attacked the British front south of the Somme, and breaking through the line at Villers-Bretonneux succeeded in capturing the town. That same night the 13th and 15th Brigades counter-attacked and regained Villers-Bretonneux before daybreak of the following morning.

The day of the 26th was spent by the Battalion in much the same spirit of expectancy, and then orders were received that it should relieve a unit of the 13th Brigade on the following night. This was changed several times. The following morning brought more changes of destination and of work; and when the Battalion finally left Pont Noyelles at night, it made no use of the 'buses but marched to a place six miles further south. This was Cachy, a village less than two miles west of Villers-Bretonneux. There the unit relieved British troops.

In the position which the Battalion now occupied it was in touch with French troops on its right, whilst it had the 47th Battalion on its left flank. Opposite the line and but a short distance below the southern outskirts of Villers-Bretonneux, a chateau stood on high ground and surrounded by a thick belt of timber. The place was known as Monument Wood, and was considered to give a dominating advantage to the enemy. The high ground afforded him a good view of the country in front. All work done on the Australian lines had been done at night, as the observation from Monument Wood made impossible work by day. Yet perhaps the greatest danger to Australian troops afforded by Monument Wood was the temptation it offered for attack.

An attack on Monument Wood was decided for the 3rd of May. There was little time for the incoming unit to do more than make the necessary preparations. The construction of forward dumps of ammunition, flares, reserves of drinking water, and the making of careful reconnaissance could be accomplished only at night.

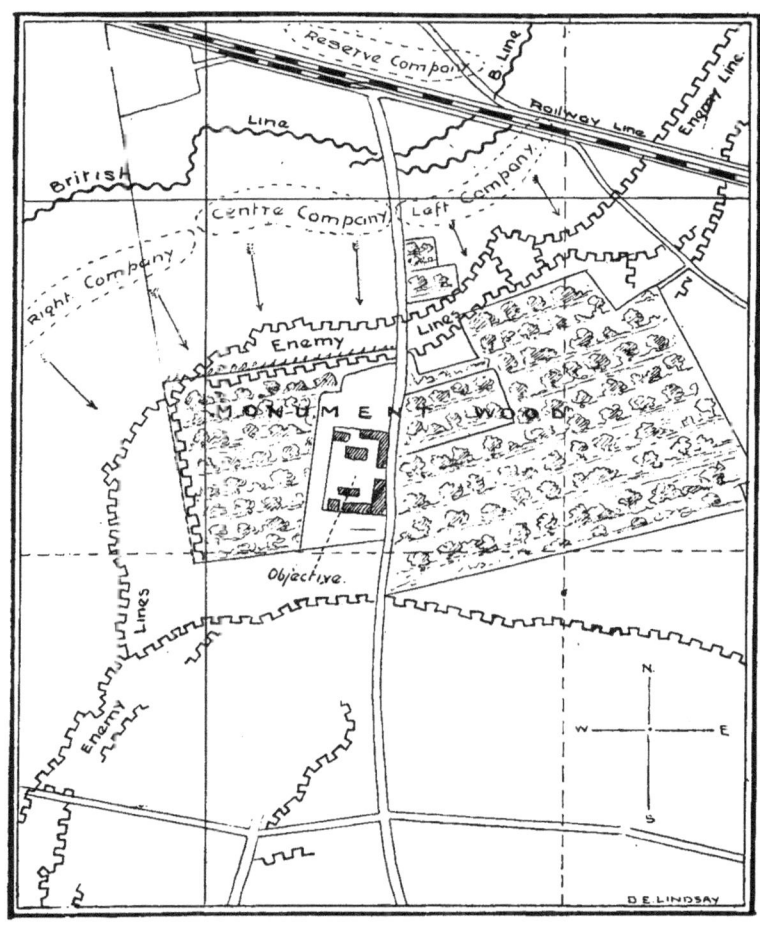

Map showing the Battalion's Assault on Monument Wood (drawn to scale).

At that time the British front line ran due north and south on the east side of Villers-Bretonneux cutting the main railway line that connects Villers-Bretonneux with Amiens. When it crossed to the south side of the railway line, it ran roughly parallel with the railway for some distance and then gradually veered towards the south. The Germans occupied formidable entrenchments along the fringe of the wood, protected by heavy wire entanglements. The whole position seemed from the subsequent fire to be a nest of machine-guns.

The 45th Battalion was holding that part of the line from which the attack was to be launched. On the night preceding the attack the 48th troops moved forward to the jumping-off trench. The strength of the unit was at this time twenty-seven officers and six hundred and sixty-five of other ranks, and before 2 o'clock on the morning of the 3rd the attacking troops were in position.

At 2 a.m. our artillery opened fire, and after a preliminary bombardment lasting two minutes the 48th advanced to the attack. Three companies took part in the assault, followed by a mopping-up party composed of three officers and fifty of other ranks drawn from the fourth company which was held in reserve. The companies began to advance on an even front. The machine-gun fire with which the enemy met them soon showed plainly that little or inadequate damage had been done by our artillery. Captain Imlay, commanding the left company, fell badly wounded under this fire. When the company had got to the enemy's wire entanglements, it found these an insuperable obstacle except on its right flank where a party of men got through to the objective.

The inadequate artillery preparation for the task was now evident along the whole front of attack. The company in the centre made some headway but was held up by the thick wire which rendered easy victims to the heavy machine-gun fire. On the right Captain Cumming was similarly blocked by the close timber and wire. He endeavoured to clear this obstacle by leading a party around it to attack on the western side of the wood. Whilst doing so he was killed, and that attempt also ended in failure.

Better fortune attended to what might be called the informal party to the attack, the mopping-up party, though its success could not affect the general issue of the venture. This party under Lieutenant Stoerkel managed to get through a gap in the defences, and striking towards the chateau captured a German officer and twenty of other ranks.

Meanwhile daylight had come and tanks then went forward against the enemy's machine-gun positions. One of these fell into a German trench, and becoming inoperative its crew was captured. Later in the day it was destroyed by our artillery. The other tanks did good work, but they had entered the fighting at a time when the striking force of the infantry was already spent.

An attempt was made to form a line which, whilst embracing ground far short of the objective originally intended, should secure something in return for the day's losses. Before this could be consolidated the enemy made a strong counter-attack, which forced our troops back to the original line.

Twenty-one German prisoners represented the fruits of the day's attack on Monument Wood. On the other hand the Battalion's casualties amounted to nine officers and one hundred and fifty of other ranks, and indeed this total was a small one considering the magnitude of the task. The facility of wisdom after the event is proverbial; and even now it would be difficult to judge rightly from the opinion of the unit concerned the effect of a particular incident on the general result. At the time, however, it was considered an unfortunate undertaking, wherein success would scarcely have justified the sacrifice that failure made a tragedy.

CHAPTER XIX.

THE STRAIN LIGHTENS.

ON the night following the assault on Monument Wood, the Battalion left the front line and went back to Blangy-Tronville, a village about four miles further west. Here the men could enjoy some rest as the enemy was not then shelling the area. It was well within range of the enemy's guns, however, so a position had to be chosen in trenches near at hand to which the troops could retire in case the village was shelled. A miserable wet night was spent in those trenches on the 6th. Intelligence reports had anticipated an attack by the enemy which was understood should be preceded by a bombardment of Blangy-Tronville. All ranks were ordered from the village and had to take shelter in the trenches. No shells landed in the village; but in the trenches to which they had resorted several shells fell in the early morning, compelling some of the troops to seek safety in other directions.

The Battalion again went forward on the afternoon of the 7th, and took up positions on a line running behind Villers-Bretonneux and through Aubigny. There it spent two quiet days being held close at hand for any emergency that might arise. In those days the enemy was expected to attack at any time or in any place. The strenuous and persistent manner in which he had hitherto conducted his offensive, seemed to indicate that he was making a last great gamble for superiority. Therefore, although the Battalion was not at this time in the front line, vigilance was never relaxed and all ranks " stood to " at 4 o'clock each morning.

General Gellibrand having returned to the Brigade, Colonel Leane resumed command of the 48th, and on the evening of the 10th led the Battalion into the front line. There also the men had a quiet time from the enemy. Work went on as strenuously as ever, work which consisted mostly in digging, in improving defences and preparing the position to withstand better any future attack.

After four days spent in the front line the men were withdrawn to the supports where they were engaged on the same kind of work. The weather was then fine, the nights calm and well suited to aeroplane work. So whilst the men lay in support they were several times bombed from the air. Moreover the working parties employed at night in the line suffered a considerable number of casualties from machine-gun fire.

But already there were evident signs that the Germans were slackening in their offensive on the southern front of battle. When they began their great advance on the 31st of March, that advance had swept across the old battlefield of the Somme. Then ensued a period of normal trench warfare, except where strenuous local engagements were forced by the enemy with a view to securing some particular advantage and subsequently resuming the advance. It was felt that his offensive on the Somme had ceased only for the time being, and that he would spare no effort to prepare for the reopening of it.

Away to the north the enemy had delayed his attack until the fine weather dried up the wet and low lying country. There too his advance had been equally successful. The early part of April saw places in the northern sector in the hands of the Germans, that were already made familiar to the 48th Battalion by days of hard fighting around them. Thus Messines was again lost, whose capture had cost so many lives, and Wytschaete and Ploegsteert with its adjoining wood. Hollebeke, near which the Battalion had spent several weeks of the preceding winter and on whose defences it had spent much vain work in the snow and frost, was retaken by the enemy; and Passchendaele Ridge where lay so many Australian dead. Crossing the frontier into France the Germans occupied Armentières and Bailleul and Meteren and Doulieu. The great effort of the enemy seemed, however, to have reached its climax before the end of May in both northern and southern sectors. When therefore the 48th Battalion was relieved from its position in supports on the night of the 21st of May, it had completed a term of duty in which hard work had taken the place of hard fighting. It was indeed strenuous work, and as the men left the trenches they were showing all the signs of the long strain to which they had been subjected almost continuously since they left Meteren in the last week of March.

Rivery, a town lying but a short distance east of Amiens, was the destination of the Battalion, and not till 5 o'clock on the following morning did the last company of the unit arrive there. Even at that early hour the regimental band turned out to meet the party, and the men were played to their billets amidst very noisy rejoicings.

The Somme flowed near to the town and on the day following their relief all ranks had a swim, and the river carried the accumulated dirt of many days in the trenches to the sea. Bright sunny weather marked their stay in Rivery, so swimming was a general pastime. The regimental band had to work overtime, and was in constant demand during the long summer evenings. Then too the "Coo-ees," a concert-troupe belonging to the 3rd Australian Division, gave a show every night which drew large crowds.

On the first Sunday spent at Rivery, General Birdwood presented decorations to several members of the Battalion. This was his last appearance in the unit as commander of the Australian Corps, a command which he relinquished on going to the 5th British Army.

At this time all Australian units were very much reduced in strength, as the result of the heavy fighting in which they had participated. It was therefore found impossible to keep up the supply of reinforcements necessary to maintain four Battalions in each Brigade. It was decided that henceforth nearly all Brigades should have but three Battalions, and in the 12th Brigade it fell to the lot of the 47th Battalion to be disbanded. Officers and men of that Battalion were accordingly allotted among the other units of the Brigade, so good blood from Queensland and Tasmania was now added to the 48th.

At Rivery also Colonel Leane ceased to command the 48th Battalion, his place being taken by Colonel Perry. General Gellibrand was promoted to the command of the 3rd Australian Division and Colonel Leane became Brigadier. The unit was still at Rivery at the end of the month, when it received orders to return to the forward area on the 2nd of June. The Battalion went forward to a place still a considerable distance from the line, as the Brigade was being kept in reserve to the Division. It left Rivery at 5 o'clock in the morning and arrived at its destination about three hours later. The men dug positions for themselves in the face of a high bank that afforded good shelter from shell-fire. They remained there for a fortnight being employed in the usual work of troops lying in the reserve area, salvage, cable-laying, digging, training reinforcements.

On the evening of the 16th the unit set out for the front line as soon as it was sufficiently dark to permit of troops moving without observation. Its destination was Sailly-le-Sec. The congestion of traffic on the roads made the journey a tedious one, during which several casualties were sustained from the enemy's shell-fire. Although the Battalion remained in the front line for three weeks, its casualties were but fifty-three of other ranks including ten men killed. The last day of its term of duty, the 4th of July, was the occasion of a brilliant operation extending from Villers-Bretonneux to the Somme by troops of the 2nd, 3rd and 4th Australian Divisions. The 48th Battalion was able to have

THE STRAIN LIGHTENS.

a good view of the advance from the part of the line it was holding.

This operation showed that a definite change was taking place in the character of the fighting, which was no longer purely defensive on the part of the Allies. It prepared the way for the great offensive which was to begin on the following month. A week after the Australian advance at Villers-Bretonneux had taken place, the Battalion left the forward area. It went back to the district around Allonville, where it spent the remaining two weeks of July in race-meetings, sports, and every kind of enjoyment that could be organised in conjunction with the other units of the Brigade and of the Division.

Chapter XX.

TOWARDS THE EAST.

ON the 1st of August the Battalion was in billets in the eastern suburbs of deserted Amiens. A few days later it marched further east, and bivouaced in trenches not far below Corbie, but on the left side of the river Somme. Except that a great attack was impending, little was known. But further to the east of them lay the country around Hamel, where other Australian units had met with great success in the previous month, and where minor operations had since taken place to prepare for the subsequent development of that success. That the time had now arrived for its development was rightly guessed by all ranks, whilst the preparations being made for it indicated that the attack was to take place on a large scale.

It is interesting to note the stores which the Battalion was instructed to draw for that operation : 45,000 rounds of small arms ammunition ; 1000 Mill's grenades, No. 36 ; 500 Mill's grenades, No. 5 ; 250 Mill's grenades, No. 27 ; an additional water-bottle and carrier for all ranks ; 280 ground flares ; 200 refills for Tommy-cookers and the usual emergency rations ; 8 pack-saddles ; 8 water-tin carriers ; 10 message rockets. Besides these there were allotted to the Battalion two supply tanks, which were to make a double trip to it on the day of the engagement, carrying fifty petrol-tins of water as well as ammunition. On the evening before the attack these supply-tanks were set afire by enemy shells and their dangerous cargo completed their destruction, so that other arrangements had to be made.

The proposed advance, which was to be a simultaneous operation of units of the Fourth Army extended over a wide front, was to be made in three successive waves. In that part of the front of attack which most concerned the 48th Battalion, troops of the 3rd Australian Division were holding the line. These were to attack from a jumping-off trench but a short distance in front of the line they occupied, and advance to the first objective about three and a quarter miles distant. The 45th and 46th Battalions were to pass through these troops at a fixed time after zero hour, whilst the 48th Battalion was to follow over the occupied ground at a measured distance behind them and be ready to attack towards the final objective. Troops of the 5th Australian Division were to operate on their right with Canadian troops, whilst other Australian units were to be on their immediate left with English troops further north of them.

The attack was expected to take place at an early date, but only at 6 o'clock on the evening of the 7th was the Battalion notified that zero hour would be 4.20 of the following morning. The Brigade was then several miles behind the front line, and during the early morning moved forward to be within easy reach of the place where it was to begin its work.

At 4.20 a.m. the guns, many of them hitherto silent and concealed, opened fire and as the morning was still rather dark the flashes of the batteries seemed to set the whole area ablaze. The enemy's retaliation was at first very light, and everything pointed to the attack having been a complete surprise.

An hour later the 48th Battalion started from its position about two miles behind the original front line. Keeping direction with difficulty in the heavy fog and smoke, it got to the other side of Accroche Wood in front of which was its first assembly-point. Nine fighting-tanks were to co-operate with the Battalion; but before this point was reached one of them had been ditched, whilst another was struck by a shell which killed a Lewis-gunner of the 48th who was riding on it, and wounded an officer and two of other ranks.

In this sector thick wooded spurs were numerous, Rat Wood, Hazel Wood, Jean Wood, Richmond Wood, with deep ravines adjoining or running through them that made the ground very difficult. The avoidance of these obstacles necessitated long detours for the tanks, and occasioned their subsequent failure to give effective co-operation.

The negotiation of those same spurs and ravines made tedious work for the infantry, but fortunately the pace of the Battalion required to be a slow one to allow of the preceding stages in the advance being accomplished. The journey forward therefore was not too strenuous, except on the high ground when the scattered artillery-fire of the enemy made it prudent to hurry to the next ravine. In the shelter of one such ravine forward of Rat Wood the men had a prolonged halt, and as the early morning had put appetites on edge all sat down to bully-beef and biscuits with much relish. Whilst so engaged a low-flying enemy aeroplane swooped over and fired its machine-gun on them, but did not inflict any casualties.

The journey over the newly captured ground was an interesting one. Tanks were rumbling forward by many different routes. A battery of Royal Horse Artillery galloping into action, unlimbering, firing several rounds and again galloping forward, presented a sight not often witnessed in what had hitherto been a campaign of almost continuous trench-war. Here on the low ground near Rat Wood lay several of the enemy's guns, the first fruits of the advance. Large batches of prisoners were passing to the rear, some carrying wounded Australians, others themselves wounded and being helped along painfully by their comrades.

As the Battalion again advanced it was under direct observation from an observation-balloon, which the enemy had sent up immediately the fog cleared sufficiently to afford visibility. There was much relief when one of our aeroplanes darted towards it and set it afire. When the troops had got

"In the shelter of one such ravine . . . the men had a prolonged halt, . . . Whilst so engaged, a low-flying enemy aeroplane swooped over and fired its machine-gun on them . . . ."

to the high ground beyond Jean Wood, they suddenly found themselves under the machine-gun fire of the enemy. The Battalion Commander received a bullet-wound in his arm but the wound was not serious and all hurried towards the gully adjoining Richmond Wood. There more of the tanks that were following them were thrown out of action by the difficult ground.

It was now about 10.30 a.m. and the Battalion was close to the second objective, where the preceding troops had made good their position. Final arrangements were made for the advance to the third objective, and the companies were disposed in the manner that had already been determined, A Company on the right, C in the centre, and D on the left, whilst B Company was to remain in reserve. Only three of the nine tanks allotted to the Battalion had as yet reached the line from which the third attack was to take place, but it was decided to make no further delay, and at 11 o'clock the companies advanced towards the final objective.

The company on the right had rapid success, and after about an hour's fighting established its position. The troops in the centre and on the left met with much stronger resistance, and suffered rather heavy casualties from machine-gun fire. One of the tanks reached the opposing trenches in this part of the field, and was rendering good assistance when it suddenly went on fire. So the men had to fight their way as best they could making use of old trenches or such cover as the nature of the ground afforded, in their endeavour to get to close quarters with enemy machine-gun positions. About 12.30, however, the Battalion had gained its final objective, and was occupying a frontage of 2300 yards.

Up to this time one hundred and nine prisoners had been taken, including five officers. The area also yielded some booty, twenty light and heavy machine-guns and two anti-tank guns being captured in it. The village of Proyart lay just ahead, where the enemy could be seen very active in its streets.

One rather pathetic picture, affording good evidence that it was not expected the attack should be pushed so far, was presented by a German waggon drawn up close to what must recently have been the headquarters of a unit. It was that source of interest and pleasure to all troops, the mail-cart just arrived that morning with the soldiers' letters and parcels. Its team of three horses fully harnessed and yoked lay on the ground with their driver beside them, having been caught by one of our shells even as they hastened away. Some hurried attempt must have been made to save the mails, for the contents of the mail-bags were strewn over the road. The soldier, be he digger or Fritz, is a "sentimental bloke" and the rude scatterment of home news and affectionate trifles was a sorry sight.

There were other things in abundance at those headquarters. Cigarettes that were not the unpopular brand which the German soldier is wont to smoke, for they had come from English canteens. And matches, which were then almost unprocurable but with which the same source had liberally supplied the recently advancing enemy. There was wine also, and cognac, and huge casks of beer, and other supplies which grew progressively as the news of them was carried back to the rear; until those troops who had taken the first objective, and the second objective, felt aggrieved that they had not also been allowed to take the third objective.

If such luxuries were in strong contrast to the rather spartan fare of an Australian headquarters in the field, equally so was the abominable filth of the place. The enemy had no elaborate dug-outs here, but had erected substantial shelters on the face of a ridge. It was evidently an artillery headquarters, and stables were everywhere. They adjoined the shelters, their refuse was banked up against the living quarters, and was copiously used to camouflage them from aeroplane observation. Latrines were erected without any attempt at either privacy or sanitation. On that warm sunny day the flies swarmed over the dead, swarmed over clots of blood on the ground, over food, over everything. The whole scene told its own tale; either the enemy had been too rapid in his success to be organized, or he had become too disorganized to be any longer successful. It looked like the beginning of the end.

The enemy made no attempt to counter-attack and the night passed without incident. But by next morning some light guns were firing from the other side of Proyart, and a heavy battery also was ranging on the newly occupied position. From this onward the enemy's shelling grew more intense, and added considerably to the small list of casualties sustained in the advance itself. The troops on the right of the Battalion had pushed forward about eight hundred yards to secure a minor improvement of the position. So on the night of the 9th the 48th swung its right flank into line with them. Except for this change no further advance was attempted. Fighting patrols were sent out towards Proyart, but the village was found to be too strongly held to enter without artillery preparation and support.

On the following day the Battalion could watch the advance on their more remote left, where English troops had had a hard task on the 8th over the extremely difficult ground. Australian and American troops were now attempting it, and every one was much interested, for the Yanks were then little known to the Battalion. But the heavy smoke barrage obscured everything, and little could be seen except the winding progress of the tanks and small groups of men on the high ridges.

Late that night the Battalion was relieved amidst rather heavy shelling which inflicted some half-dozen casualties, and the men made their way back over the captured ground. Enemy bombing 'planes were active, and were following the line of the main road which ran straight as an arrow between Amiens and St. Quentin. But the troops gave the road a wide berth, and keeping to the open country continued back beyond the line which had marked the first objective of the advance. From there they crossed over the river Somme and came to a deep winding gully at dawn, when they threw themselves on the open ground to sleep the sleep that comes after a strenuous time in the trenches.

Where the Battalion now rested was but another part of the battle-field of the 8th. Everyone was in good spirits for the weather was warm and the Somme lay conveniently near for a swim. Moreover, the quartermaster came to light with "a clean change," something which provokes as much interest after a term in the line as does the arrival of the mail. So no one minded when the rest came to a sudden ending on the third day, and the Battalion again headed towards the battle-front.

Again the Somme was crossed and the men continued south and west, till about 1 a.m., when they bivouaced in trenches near Harbonnières. This village lay some two miles south of the position they had occupied in the advance. In the morning it was known that arrangements were being made for another advance by Australian, Canadian and French troops, in which the Battalion was to take part. Tanks were already coming up from the back area, and guns were getting into new positions. But that evening all arrangements were cancelled, and the 12th Brigade was ordered to relieve Australian troops which were then holding the line in front.

The line there lay near Lihons and looked over towards Chaulnes, and on the following night the 48th moved forward to a position in support of the Brigade. Later on it relieved the troops holding the front trenches. But throughout its term in this area the Battalion was very fortunate, and experienced a quiet time until its relief on the night of the 24th of August. The Brigade was relieved, however, by French troops, the tedious process of " taking over" was not facilitated by the slight acquaintance of the two parties to the relief with the other's language, and some movement must have been observed by the enemy which apprised him of what was taking place. So the whole forward area of the sector was literally drenched with gas-shells, and one witnessed that pitiful spectacle, men in gas-helmets blindly feeling their way through narrow communication-saps whilst constantly hampered by their equipment.

The Battalion got away safely, however, and continued towards Harbonnières which it reached about 3 a.m. There a column of motor-lorries was awaiting it, and in these it was carried away to the rest-area beyond Amiens, and arrived at its new billets in the village of St. Vast on a sleepy Sunday morning.

CHAPTER XXI.

THE BATTALION'S LAST ENGAGEMENT.

AT St. Vast the Battalion rested for nearly two weeks Meanwhile there were momentous changes on the battle-front. The attack launched on the 8th of August had placed Amiens out of the range of the enemy guns; and even as the Battalion came through the outskirts of the city on its way to the rest area, some few civilians were to be seen in its silent streets. The same attack had again opened up the railway communications between Amiens and Paris.

Other interesting things too had happened. When its brief spell after the recent advance was interrupted, and the Battalion was hurried up to Harbonnières to participate in another attack on the same front, the arrangements for that attack were suddenly cancelled. It was decided to make the advance from a front further north, and this advance began only a week later. Its series of operations, covering about ten days and which are known as the battle of Bapaume, turned the enemy's flank north of the Somme, and thus compelled him to evacuate all the area which he occupied south and west of the river. This area included the territory lying opposite the Lihons front, of which the 48th Battalion had held comparatively quiet possession during the first stages of the battle further north. It is interesting to note that the heavy gas-shelling to which he subjected the Battalion on the night they were relieved from those trenches, was the enemy's last display from that part of the front. Immediately afterwards he withdrew all his forces some nine or ten miles back to the east side of the river. Still more interesting is it that the ground opposite the same front, which was the objective of the attack primarily projected, was thus gained without a shot being fired for it.

Some master mind guided the tactics of those days, and during the Battalion's first week at St. Vast another great attack was launched still further north. This was the battle of Arras, which reached the outer defences of the Hindenburg Line. Just as the previous advance caused an evacuation of territory south of the Somme, so did this advance necessitate a retreat of the enemy in the far north which soon became a rout. In the British sector on the western front contact had now been made with the northern part of the enemy's last great line of strongholds, the main Hindenburg Line. On its southern end the outer system of that line had as yet to be broken. One great battle was still to be fought to prepare the way for the attack on the main line which, as the future was to prove, should result in the enemy seeing the futility of further opposition.

The 48th Battalion concerned itself very little with these matters during its stay at St. Vast. Intelligence reports occasionally came to the unit and were posted on the notice-board for the information of the men. The digger, however, has a shrewd standard of the value of intelligence reports. The number of prisoners taken is the hard and fast rule by which he judges them and the only item that interests him. He had other interests with which to concern himself during those days. For the Brigade had now its own pierrot troupe, which was touring the Brigade area. Then there was some hope of a race-meeting at an early date, though Divisional headquarters was said to look with an unfavourable eye on the sport because of the abuse of horse-flesh which it entailed. But a very successful Brigade sports-meeting was held, at which some of the soldiers acted as bookmakers and book-makers' clerks. They were able to appear in what is regarded as the characteristic attire of their colleagues in civil life, by borrowing various garments from the French people of the neighbourhood.

On the 7th of September they left St. Vast, and were again carried on motor-lorries past Amiens and through the recently evacuated area to Barleux, a place some distance south-west of Peronne. There they bivouaced for the night in the trenches. Two days later they marched to Catelet and on the following day to Beaumetz. Next night they spent a very miserable time in the rain amidst the ruins of Flechin.

Flechin was still some miles behind the front line, but the unit lay near a road along which passed much of the traffic of preparation for the coming battle. The weather again became fine, with bright sunny days and clear moonlight nights. In the daytime the road was very quiet. During the night, however, it presented a scene of activity common to the eve of every great attack, but ever unfailing in its interest. Giant howitzers drawn by traction-engines, batteries with their six-horse teams, motor-lorries and ammunition-waggons, went along in a seemingly endless line. Here and there a first-line transport hurried to its battalion in the trenches with rations and water, or a section of ammunition-limbers with shells to their field-batteries. Their Australian drivers, ever ready to take a risk, would whip their teams into a mad canter, double-banking on the column in an effort to get ahead, whilst the watching infantrymen would applaud and bet with one another on the chances of a block in the traffic or of a lorry getting ditched ; and the outraged traffic-control would shout violent oaths of vengeance on the offenders, until he spluttered and choked with the dust that soared aloft obscuring the light of the moon.

No one can ever forget the strenuous fulness of that life, which the infantryman often saw whilst making his way forward to play his own surpassing part in it. No one can ever forget the reckless vigour of it, its manly risks, its noisy strife and its weird language.

After spending five days at Flechin the Battalion moved up to the front line on the night of the 16th, and relieved the troops occupying it. The immediate front was not held by a continuous trench but by outposts, which were manned by A Company and half of another company, whilst the remainder of the Battalion took up a position in the support trenches. The relief was completed before midnight, and all went quietly for about an hour. Then a heavy storm broke over the area, thunder drowned the noise of what few guns were firing and a great downpour of rain followed.

Next day weather conditions were better, and arrangements were finalised for the Battalion's part in the advance. So far as the Brigade sector was concerned, it presented much the same features as that of the advance on the 8th of August; except that the 48th Battalion was on this occasion to advance to the first objective, whilst the second objective was allotted to the 45th and the third to the 46th Battalion. Other units of the 4th Australian Division were to advance on the left of the Brigade, with the 1st Australian Division again on their left. English troops were to advance on the right flank of the Brigade sector. Zero hour was finally known to be at 5.20 on the following morning.

On the morning of the 18th, the men were withdrawn from the out-posts about half-an-hour before zero hour and at 5 a.m. the companies were in position on the jumping-off tape with B on the left, D in the centre and C on the right, whilst A Company was to follow in close support. Falling rain made the morning quite dark and very gloomy. One tank was allotted for work in the Brigade sector, but early in the advance it got too far to the right and was not seen again. A dummy tank, however, a canvas-covered framework making a fair representation of a tank viewed from a distance, was drawn to the tape-line by a reluctant mule. Unfortunately the mule soon made for a heavy belt of wire, where the "tank" immediately became inoperative after the fashion of tanks.

At 5.20 a.m. the barrage fell, and as it gradually advanced the infantry started forward keeping pace with it. The enemy's artillery retaliation was very light, although some casualties were sustained before the troops left the jumping-off trench. Little opposition was encountered from those who were occupying his advance outposts. The latter were the first prisoners of the advance, but after their surrender the Battalion's task became more difficult. Between it and its objective was a well dug trench which seemed to be full of troops. On the side of the trench which lay towards the right wing of the Brigade sector, several large dug-outs were afterwards discovered. In these the enemy had evidently taken refuge whilst the artillery played on that part of the field. But as soon as the barrage had gone forward, the garrison immediately showed themselves very active against the advancing troops. From the high ground on the right side of the trench, they began to direct machine-gun fire on the men advancing on the left wing of the Brigade front.

The company of the 48th which was operating on the right got into the trench and began bombing its way along it. In this manner our troops drove a great part of its garrison into corners where they surrendered, or into its roomy dug-outs only to surrender later on. From these dug-outs, where one could see the remains of an interrupted breakfast strewn over the place, over seventy prisoners were taken, and altogether one hundred and twenty prisoners were captured in this trench. The number did not represent all the forces which a few minutes before had here opposed the Battalion. The remainder had run to the hollow on the other side of the rising ground, and most of them took up a position along a sunken road there. Others sought refuge in a large dug-out which was evidently an enemy headquarters. Their plight was a sorry one on the sunken road, for they were right on our

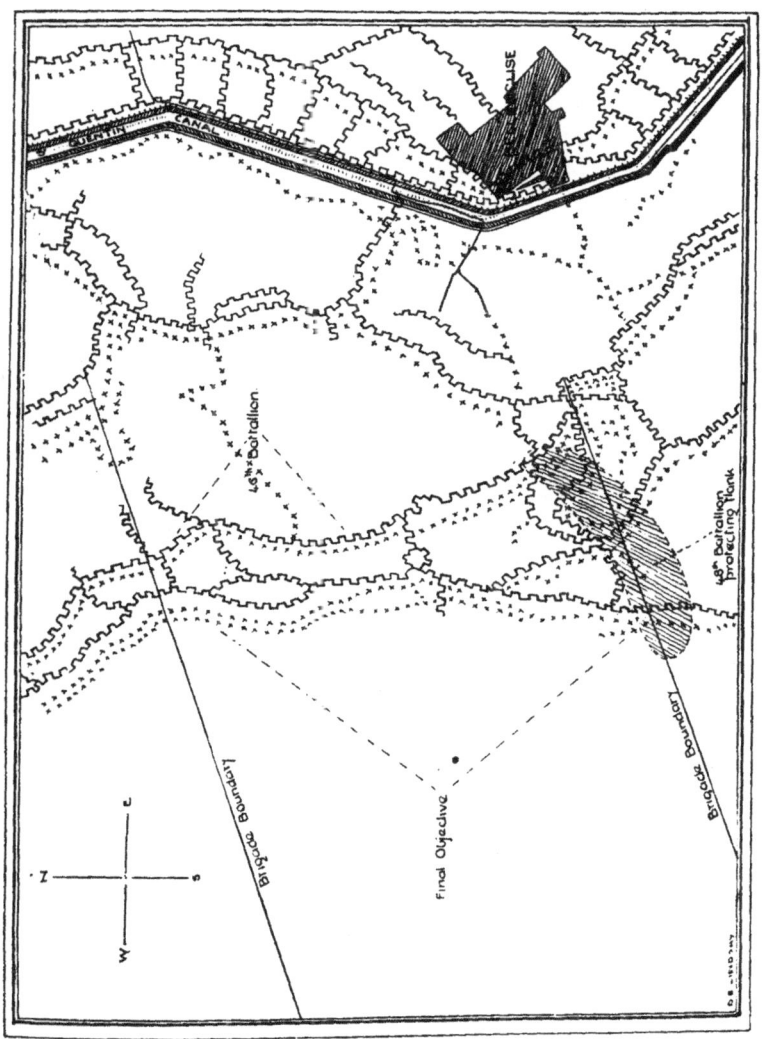

Map showing the Battalion's position in the outer defences of the Hindenburg Line (drawn to scale).

Facing p. 146.

artillery's protective barrage line. More enemy dead were strewn over that small area than the writer of these pages had ever before seen gathered on the same extent of ground. Many of those who came under the heavy fire ran forward with hands upraised in token of surrender, and from this place and the adjoining dug-out one hundred and eighty-nine prisoners were taken including eleven officers. Like other Australian battalions, it was many days since the 48th had gone into action with more than half its establishment of men. Yet in this engagement altogether some 480 prisoners were taken, and the objective was reached with very few casualties to the attacking troops.

The 45th Battalion now passed through the troops of the 48th and secured the second objective with another large batch of prisoners, then finally the 46th in turn advanced towards the final objective. But now things were not so happy with the troops attacking on the right flank of the Brigade sector. They had been held up by a small village some distance ahead of their second objective. The 46th Battalion was therefore compelled to take up a position on a sunken road, to the west of the formidable system of trenches whose occupation was the Brigade's final objective. At night the same Battalion secured that objective, whilst capturing more prisoners than the number of troops employed in the operation. It subsequently transpired that this capture was made from a fresh unit, which had come to the trenches an hour previously, and the prisoners were thus out of action almost before they had fired a shot.

The troops on the right of the Brigade sector had not secured their final objective, so a company of the 48th was sent forward to form a protecting flank to the 46th Battalion, whose right flank was now in the air. Henceforward the severest fighting was transferred to this flank. The small hours of the morning of the 19th were spent in trying to link up with the troops on the right, and prevent a flank attack of the enemy from that direction.

To the right and rear of the Brigade's final objective was a formidable enemy strong-point, from which machine-guns commanded a wide field of fire in various directions. It was shortly after they had gone forward and whilst endeavouring to find some system in the maze of trenches, that a number of 48th men encountered this obstacle. It required concentrated and careful attack and help was summoned from the troops reconnoitring other parts of the position. Meanwhile one firebrand, a lad named Woods, hoisted himself on the parapet of a neighbouring trench. He was soon the aim of many bullets; but the fortune of war, as remarkable in its friendships as it is in its spites, dealt kindly with him. Lying on his stomach whilst his comrades below "fed him" with bombs, he created such havoc in the strong-point that when reinforcements arrived their task was an easy one. Thus was the 48th Battalion awarded its first Victoria Cross in what was to be its last engagement.

The fight continued till dawn, the same trench being occupied by the 48th on the left and by the enemy on the right. Right and left and right and left it swayed, our troops hurriedly building rough obstacles in the trenches with loose wire, old machine-guns or any of the débris that strews a battlefield and that might serve to block or retard the enemy in his next sally. The struggle dragged on and on with increasing bitterness, until the fight in the darkness lost the dignity of battle and there was enacted something more crude and savage than mere warfare. But ever each fresh repulse saw the blocks in the trenches carried further to the right, and the enemy pressed further down the sloping ground, until dawn came and the position was for the time being secure.

On the night of the 20th two companies of the Battalion took over part of the front line, and on the following day moved forward to positions on the right which established the defence of that flank on a more definite system. There they could see the fruits of their victory, for right ahead of them lay the St. Quentin Canal, the village of Bellenglise and the imposing structure of the main Hindenburg Line. The battle had been fought and won, which prepared the way for the great assault that was to be almost the end of the struggle.

The protecting flank, however, had cost the Battalion dearly. Far more casualties were sustained in the fighting for that bit of ground, and in the subsequent heavy shelling of it, than had been suffered in the unit's previous advance. Lieutenant Ward was killed there, and several men long associated with the Battalion.

There too, poor Lunt was killed, the best known man in the Battalion and the hero of many fights both in the line and out of it, for he gave as much trouble to his friends as he did to the enemy. With Punch Donovan and Cork Daly and some others, he formed a small party that one learned to look on as essential to the identity of the 48th. Throughout its career, from Pozières to Bellenglise, they might be seen supplying their comic relief to the tragedy of every engagement. Colonels and adjutants might come and go, but it almost seemed that they must continue while the Battalion lasted. Always conspicuous in an attack, but as soon as the climax of that excitement had passed they sought fresh interest in the odd jobs that ensued from it. If prisoners were to be taken to the rear, the duty of escort was regarded as theirs by right, and many were the antics with which they performed the task. They knew everything for they were everywhere, and seemed to have no regular duty but to be the emergency men of the unit. They received decorations, and none were better deserved, but the same gipsy character which made them so useful to the Battalion as regular and irregular scouts, made promotion impossible. Authority was prudently tolerant of the latitude they gave themselves, and they seemed to want no further favour.

Lunt's career with the 48th came to an end opposite Bellenglise, and his comrades buried him and those who had fallen with him. Fortunately they were not too many. When, however, at a future date hostilities ceased, and it was known that the unit had seen its last fight, the knowledge gave a retrospective pathos to the fate of those poor fellows who fell so near to final victory. Down by the small spur known as Dean Copse some of them were laid to rest, men who had fallen in the first stage of the advance. Further up on the face of the hill another plot received the men who died when the 48th made its last stand, and also their comrades of the other Battalions who had fallen in the progress of that last advance of the Brigade.

"Down by the small spur known as Dean Copse some of them were laid to rest. . . . ."

Chapter XXII.

THE DAYS OF THE ARMISTICE.

THE Battalion left the front line to set out for the rest-area. Making several stages on the journey, it went part of the way on foot, part by 'bus, until it arrived at Revelles, a village lying west of Amiens. There the unit settled down in billets at the end of September, and remained throughout the following month.

Hard training went on all the time. The long promised war of movement was supposed to have definitely begun, and the character of the training was modified accordingly. Recreation was given its due place, however, and sports-meetings were frequently held. A large wooden concert-hall was erected in one of the villages of the area, where troupes from different units regularly gave entertainments.

Meanwhile affairs in the war zone were moving very rapidly. On the 27th of September two British Armies, in which many Canadian Divisions were included, had begun the operation that resulted in the capture of the Hindenburg Line. Two days later the main attack was launched, the Fourth British Army taking part in it as well as French and American Divisions. The Fifth and Third Australian Divisions attached to the Fourth Army played a conspicuous part in the fighting. The artillery of the Fourth Australian Division was engaged, but its infantry was not represented except by those officers and non-commissioned officers who were temporarily attached to an American Division for the attack. In the battle which lasted for nine days all the main

Hindenburg defences were occupied, and this line definitely broken whose intactness had become so identified with the enemy's hope of final success. The Australian Divisions engaged in the advance went back to the rest-area, and henceforth the war had finished for Australian infantry.

At the same time a heavy blow was dealt the enemy in the North. A force composed of the Belgian Army, French Divisions and some British units of the Second Army, under the command of the King of the Belgians, began an assault on the Flanders front. The enemy there held his positions lightly, and the operation proved an easy success. It involved the recapture of many old positions lost in the spring, and the withdrawal of the enemy from Lens and Armentières.

To the members of the 48th Battalion, this shifting of the battle-front eastward now became a matter of first interest. Few details concerning the fighting found their way back to the units isolated in the quiet country villages west of Amiens. Such salient facts as the intelligence reports contained were sceptically considered and debated by the diggers. The number of prisoners stated as captured were, however, regarded as definite indication of success. By the middle of October Lille was evacuated by the enemy, and henceforth the ever shifting flags on the war map registered withdrawal after withdrawal.

The beginning of November found the Australians speculating as to when this phenomenal good luck and facile success was going to cease, anticipating that its cessation would put an abrupt period to their rest. It was rumoured even then that the Germans had reached a line in which they were determined to make a stand, and that the Australian Corps would soon be in action again. The Australian Corps commander visited the area and addressed the troops of the 48th Battalion to that effect.

On the 8th of the month it was announced that the Fourth Australian Division was to proceed to the front area by train and 'bus. Orders received by the 48th Battalion were to the effect that it should entrain on the following day at 8 o'clock in the evening. Further instructions contained a postponement of the departure for twenty-four hours.

Immediately the rumour began to spread that the enemy had applied for an armistice. No better confirmation of the rumour could be obtained, however, than an ardent wish among the French civilians that it should be true. In several villages in the area the estaminet proprietors dispensed lavish hospitality to the diggers on the strength of it. The sceptical diggers, long dead to false hopes, were convinced the armistice was still a future event but quite willing to anticipate its celebration.

The Battalion was now due to entrain at 10 o'clock on the night of the 10th, but at 2 o'clock in the afternoon there was another postponement for eighteen hours, and later on for thirty-four hours. The rumours concerning the armistice began to get very definite. The French people could talk of nothing else. Amiens was supposed to be madly excited. Individual members of the Battalion stole away from the unit and set out for the city to obtain more definite information. These unofficial ambassadors were so enthused by what they saw and heard as to forget all about the responsibility of their mission. They were picked up by the military police, and detained by them whilst the diggers at Revelles were celebrating the official announcement that hostilities should cease on the following day.

The projected movement of the Australian troops was not cancelled, but during the next two days there were again several postponements. The enemy's slow-action mines were just then causing great destruction of railway bridges and roads, and thus continually upsetting all calculation of transport.

At 10 o'clock on the night of the 13th the Battalion entrained, and arriving at Epehy next morning marched immediately to Templeux le Grand. There it again entrained and went to Brancourt. The route lay through the Hindenburg Line, and a good view was obtainable of its formidable defences from the open trucks in which the Battalion was carried. On the same day the men marched to Fresnoy le Grand, a large town to which the French refugees were then gradually returning.

It was announced that at least two Australian Divisions should form part of the British Army of Occupation in Germany, and as the Fourth Division was to be one of them there was great preparation in the 48th Battalion. All the ceremonial of military life was enacted with an exactitude very unusual in campaigning units, cleaning and polishing of uniforms and equipment was insisted on, and the strictest attention to military discipline enforced. A week later there was a rumour that no Australian Division was going to Germany. Many were indignant and the rumoured alteration in the arrangements was bitterly commented on ; others casually said that they were not sorry if it put an end to " the spit-and-polish" règime.

At the same time the Battalion set out from Fresnoy le Grand, and began a long journey north and east through France. It stopped at several villages on the way, spending a night here, a few days there, and crossing the frontier into Belgium marched towards the river Meuse. In Waulsort, a pretty village on the banks of the river, it settled down towards the end of December to spend the few remaining weeks of its existence as a unit.

. . . .

It were vain to follow further the fortunes of the 48th Battalion. It would be but a narration of the commonplace, the commonplace of demobilisation. Moreover it would not be the story of the 48th. For the 48th was daily losing its identity. Gone was the old life, with its friendships formed by danger and so often broken by death. Now many were beginning to feel that its excitements, its hardships, its fatigues, its risks, were the very things that made military life tolerable. The few remaining old hands of the Battalion, men who had seen service in 1914, in early 1915, were shouldering their packs for the last time and setting out for home. The methods of demobilisation admitted of no spectacular disbanding. Every fortnight saw small drafts of men trudge off without formality to join the train that should carry them to the French coast. Away they went, to be once more miners or farmers or clerks or mere drifters on the sea of life. But they who remained to see those first drafts leave felt that the spirit of a fuller life went with them, and that the story of a battalion was told.

APPENDIX I.

GENERAL BIRDWOOD'S MESSAGE TO 48TH BATTALION.

It has been my great privilege and honour to serve with the A.I.F. since its formation, and during that long period of stress and hardship, it is only natural that with my appreciation of their fine qualities, I have developed an affection for the Australian soldiers which is deep and lasting. This long and close association with them has enabled me to appraise at its true worth their loyal comradeship—which in their successful military career has been no less conspicuous than their indomitable valour and determination. I feel I can say that at the root of many individual and collective acts of bravery is their unwritten law never to leave a mate who is in a tight place.

I take this opportunity of wishing all prosperity and happiness to my comrades of the 48th Battalion on their return to their homes in Australia. In their willing response to the call of country, and their supreme self-sacrifice in the hours of emergency, they have displayed a patriotism which stamps them with the hallmark of true citizenship. In their discharge of these responsibilities, I am confident that the honour and traditions of their Battalion will be a dominant factor in guiding them to success.

W. R. Birdwood.

General.

1st March, 1919.

APPENDIX II.

"OUR DEAD."

Reg'tl. No.	Rank	and Name.	Nature of Casualty.	Date.
3285	Pte.	Mead, W. E.	Died of Illness	9/4/16
4258	,,	Connor, M.	,, ,,	18/6/16
1662	,,	Farrell, T.	,, ,,	10/6/16
4328	,,	Randell, H. S.	Killed in Action	8/7/16
—	2nd Lt.	Hawke, S. S.	,, ,,	5/8/16
—	,,	Ottaway, H. W.	,, ,,	,,
4764	Pte.	Bourne, H. W.	Died of Wounds	10/8/16
—	2nd Lt.	Walter, W. G. A.	Killed in Action	5/8/16
—	Lieut.	Dyke, G. C.	,, ,,	7/8/16
3296	Pte.	Olliver, A. R.	Died of Wounds	12/8/16
—	2nd Lt.	Cosson, J. G.	Killed in Action	7/8/16
—	,,	Richardson, O. V.	,, ,,	9/8/16
2894 2896	} Pte.	Head, J.	Died of Wounds	7/8/16
4826	,,	Harris, T.	Killed in Action	6/8/16
2293	,,	Gould, J.	,, ,,	,,
4450	,,	Grace, M. J.	,, ,,	,,
3108	L. Cpl.	Freeman, F.	,, ,,	,,
2208	Cpl.	Mountain, S. C.	Died of Illness	23/8/16
3045	Pte.	French, J. R.	Died of Wounds	29/8/16
4427	,,	Urch, G.	Killed in Action	6/8/16
4351	,,	Vaughan, W. G.	,, ,,	,,
4922	,,	Tolano, P.	,, ,,	,,
3692	,,	Everatt, J. H.	,, ,,	5/8/16
3688	L. Cpl.	Coulls, W. A.	,, ,,	,,
4131	,,	Birt, H. W.	,, ,,	6/8/16
2617	Pte.	Bawden, S. J.	,, ,,	7/8/16
4129	,,	Barnfather, E. J.	,, ,,	,,
1721	,,	Giles, F.	,, ,,	5/8/16
2912	,,	Moyse, S. E.	,, ,,	6/8/16
4846	,,	Kilby, R.	,, ,,	8/8/16
4176	Sgt.	Nalty, T. N.	,, ,,	5/8/16
3831	Pte.	Gaskill, Q. E.	,, ,,	6/8/16
2673	L. Cpl.	Lenton, T. S.	,, ,,	5/8/16
3383	Sgt.	Revell, W. H.	,, ,,	7/8/16

"OUR DEAD."

Reg'tl. No.	Rank	Name	Nature of Casualty	Date
1600	L. Cpl.	CARR, A.	Killed in Action	7/8/16
4967	Pte.	DUNSTAN, E. J.	,, ,,	6/8/16
5050	,,	BARR, A. G.	,, ,,	,,
5063	,,	BOLE, H.	,, ,,	7/8/16
2647	L. Cpl.	CRAWFORD, S. A.	,, ,,	7/8/16
4787	Pte.	COLGAN, C.	,, ,,	8/8/16
2947	,,	WIRTA, T. O. R.	,, ,,	,,
1970	,,	BARTHOLOMAEUS, E. L.	,, ,,	,,
5043	,,	ANDERSON, H. J.	,, ,,	8/8/16
3302	,,	WANDLESS, T. H.	,, ,,	6/8/16
1741	,,	HEGARTY, F. M.	,, ,,	8/8/16
1727a	,,	GOLDSWORTHY, R. J.	,, ,,	,,
2620	L. Cpl.	FRECKLETON, F.	,, ,,	,,
2593	Pte.	DAY, M. C.	,, ,,	,,
1697	,,	CRABB, H. G.	,, ,,	,,
2270	,,	BROCKHOFF, A. G.	,, ,,	6/8/16
4642	,,	KING, A. A.	,, ,,	8/8/16
5126	,,	KINDRED, P. H.	,, ,,	,,
4296	,,	JONES, H. W.	,, ,,	,,
2294	,,	HAY, J.	,, ,,	,,
4819	,,	GEDDES, J. R.	,, ,,	,,
4814	,,	FLYNN, J. P.	,, ,,	,,
4589	,,	CUMMING, H.	,, ,,	,,
4774	,,	CRUMP, J.	,, ,,	,,
4768	,,	BRAMWELL, W.	,, ,,	,,
4253	,,	BINGHAM, E.	,, ,,	,,
4272	,,	FISHER, W. S.	,, ,,	6/8/16
4377	Cpl.	NENKE, S. B.	,, ,,	7/8/16
5128	Pte.	KNIGHT, P. H.	,, ,,	,,
4665	,,	McKENNA, W. W.	,, ,,	,,
2272	L. Cpl.	COPPIN, J.	,, ,,	6/8/16
3925	Pte.	RAMSHAW, J.	,, ,,	,,
3037	L. Cpl.	DEEVY, J.	,, ,,	,,
473	Pte.	MINETER, M.	,, ,,	5/8/16
4386	Cpl.	SIMPSON, W. J.	,, ,,	7/8/16
2607	,,	SHINN, J. W.	,, ,,	,,
4688	Pte.	PADLEY, J. W.	,, ,,	,,
2695	,,	RANDLE, J.	,, ,,	,,
4449	,,	ROSE, J.	,, ,,	,,
2938	,,	WALKER, A.	,, ,,	6/8/16
4555	,,	ASHMORE, L.	,, ,,	,,
2936	,,	THOMAS, J. L.	,, ,,	,,
4668 / 4054	,,	McLRAN, D.	,, ,,	,,
4174	Sgt.	McKAIL, R. G.	,, ,,	,,
1731	Dvr.	MURDOCH, J. H.	,, ,,	,,
3752	Pte	REES, H.	,, ,,	,,
2900	,,	JAMES, W. A.	,, ,,	,,
4175	,,	McKELLAR, W. J.	,, ,,	,,

L

Reg'tl. No.	Rank and Name.		Nature of Casualty.	Date.
1729	Pte.	Jennings, P. A.	Killed in Action	6/8/16
3789	,,	Craig, W.	Died of Wounds	15/8/16
2084	,,	Groves, G. A. P.	,, ,,	13/8/16
4633	,,	Jackson, A. J.	,, ,,	6/8/16
—	T. Capt.	Hartley, W. G.	,, ,,	9/8/16
3066	Pte.	Ingram, J.	,, ,,	7/8/16
1826	,,	Stone, L. V.	,, ,,	15/8/16
2280	Sgt.	Williams, H. H.	,, ,,	13/8/16
3068	Pte.	Jennings, G.	,, ,,	6/8/16
2157	,,	Thomas, G.	,, ,,	7/8/16
4009	,,	Taylor, J. G.	,, ,,	,,
1671	,,	Webb, A.	,, ,,	,,
3732	,,	McAuliffe, E. D.	,, ,,	9/8/16
2305	,,	Cameron, W.	Killed in Action	7/8/16
4583	,,	Corkery, P.	,, ,,	,,
2376	,,	McNamara, S.	,, ,,	,,
342	,,	Griffiths, S. G.	,, ,,	,,
3334	,,	Foreman, G. T. R.	,, ,,	,,
4362	,,	Walker, R.	,, ,,	,,
2597	L. Cpl.	White, F. G.	,, ,,	,,
2330	Pte.	Fenwick, S. R.	,, ,,	6/8/16
1717	L. Cpl.	Ferrett, H.	,, ,,	5/8/16
4138	Pte.	Chasteauneuf, W. G.	,, ,,	7/8/16
1977	,,	Berry, F. F.	,, ,,	6/8 16
3115	,,	O'Shannessy, V.	,, ,,	7/8/16
4193	,,	Wallace, H.	,, ,,	7/8/16
2137	,,	Wallace, G. H.	,, ,,	6/8/16
1694	L. Cpl.	Cook, T. B.	,, ,,	,,
2705	Pte.	Simpson, J.	,, ,,	7/8/16
3227	L. Cpl.	Anderson, H. G.	,, ,,	6/8/16
4207 / 5207	} Pte.	Torrie, W.	,, ,,	,,
1510	,,	Painter, A. W.	,, ,,	,,
3316	C.S.M.	Stewart, W.	,, ,,	5/8/16
2854	Cpl.	Schryver, H. S.	,, ,,	6/8/16
1846	Pte.	Whitelaw, T. E.	,, ,,	8/8/16
3136	,,	Montague, A. H.	,, ,,	6/8/16
2310	,,	Codling, W. E.	,, ,,	13/8/16
4873	,,	McGrath, J.	,, ,,	6/8/16
696	,,	Sprigg, D. C.	,, ,,	8/8/16
4862	,,	Maxim, F.	,, ,,	6/8/16
3991	,,	Sansom, C. F.	,, ,,	,,
4631	,,	Jones, G.	,, ,,	,,
515	Sgt.	Godden, W. J.	,, ,,	,,
4447	Pte.	Jones, F. A.	,, ,,	,,
3101	,,	Devon, J.	,, ,,	,,
4831	,,	Hazell, C. R.	,, ,,	,,
4806	,,	Faulkner, A. W.	,, ,,	,,
4284	,,	Hoult, H.	,, ,,	,,

"OUR DEAD." 163

Reg'tl. No.	Rank and Name.		Nature of Casualty.		Date.
1456	Pte.	Burks, C. P.	Killed in Action		6/8/16
4976	,,	Hammond, H.	,,	,,	,,
2893	,,	Growo, P. C.	,,	,,	2/9/16
2891	L. Cpl.	Greenham, A. E.	,,	,,	6/8/16
5048	Pte.	Aird, A. J.	,,	,,	13/8/16
5100	,,	Gard, T. J. B.	,,	,,	6/8/16
4325	,,	Quah, W.	,,	,,	8/8/16
3079	Sgt.	Foster, R. S.	,,	,,	6/8/16
5154	Pte.	Peacock, A.	,,	,,	8/8/16
2873	Q.M.S.	Clark, A. D.	,,	,,	6/8/16
5147	Pte.	Murdoch, W. S.	,,	,,	8/8/16
3775	,,	Willard, F.	,,	,,	6/8/16
4874	,,	Monaghan, W. L.	,,	,,	8/8/16
3570	,,	Weatherall, N.	,,	,,	6/8/16
2911	,,	Moore, J. W. B. H.	,,	,,	8/8/16
4561	,,	Brennan, F. M.	,,	,,	7/8/16
5136	,,	Millman, P.	,,	,,	12/8/16
2379	L. Sgt.	Beck, C. H.	,,	,,	7/8/16
4294	Pte.	Hurleton, A.	,,	,,	,,
4566	,,	Barwell, G.	,,	,,	6/8/16
717	Cpl.	Moor, F. C.	,,	,,	7/8/16
1532	Pte.	Dickson, K. H.	,,	,,	,,
5094	,,	Fingland, W. T.	,,	,,	
4445	,,	Baker, D.	,,	,,	6/8/16
3382	Cpl.	Cooper, J. W. B.	,,	,,	7/8/16
1733	Sgt.	Hallifax, L. J.	,,	,,	15/8/16
1754	Pte.	Bradford, J.	,,	,,	7/8/16
—	2nd Lt.	Law, O. R.	,,	,,	14/8/16
4010	Pte.	Taylor, J.	,,	,,	6/8/16
—	Capt.	Evans, G. F.	,,	,,	14/8/16
4003	Pte.	Strang, R.	,,	,,	6/8/16
723	Dvr.	Huffam, L.	Died of Wounds		15/8/16
4714	Pte.	Skinner, R. T.	Killed in Action		6/8/16
4017	,,	Vernela, C. W. E.	,,	,,	5/8/16
3994	,,	Sinclair, G. A.	,,	,,	6/8/16
4028	,,	Wright, R. H.	,,	,,	5/8/16
2928	,,	Samford, W. M.	,,	,,	6/8/16
3106	,,	Fisher, O.	,,	,,	5/8/16
4696	,,	Robertson, A. G.	,,	,,	6/8/16
2592	,,	Thayne, D. M.	,,	,,	5/8/16
3032	,,	Douglas, A. L.	,,	,,	8/8/16
2820	,,	Self, R.	,,	,,	5/8/16
3039	,,	Tilbrook, G. E.	,,	,,	,,
2919	L. Cpl.	Phillips, S. G.	,,	,,	,,
4372	Pte.	Morrissey, M. R.	Died of Wounds		13/8/16
3777	,,	Woods, M. E.	Killed in Action		6/8/16
4332	,,	Rowe, F. T.	Died of Wounds		10/8/16
5129	,,	Lang, E.	Killed in Action		8/8/16
2946	,,	Wilson, W. J.	Died of Wounds		,,

L 2

Reg'tl. No.		Rank and Name.	Nature of Casualty.	Date.
4659	Pte.	MEADOWS, P.	Killed in Action	8/8/16
2404	,,	SANDO, S. J.	,, ,,	12/8/16
1792	,,	O'DEA, P. J.	,, ,,	8/8/16
2090	,,	O'RIELLY, M.	,, ,,	13/8/16
2595	,,	NOWLAND, T. H.	,, ,,	8/8/16
1710	,,	GILBERT, P. G.	,, ,,	13/8/16
3335	,,	MARTIN, D. L.	,, ,,	6/8/16
4186	,,	SMITH, P. H.	,, ,,	12/8/16
1752	,,	JOHNSON, J. T. T.	,, ,,	6/8/16
1742	,,	TAYLOR, W. H.	,, ,,	14/8/16
1775	,,	MOORE, P. V. R.	,, ,,	6/8/16
3151	,,	JOHNSON, W. A.	,, ,,	13/8/16
1052	Cpl.	JENNINGS, H. R.	,, ,,	6/8/16
4582	Pte.	CAMPBELL, J.	,, ,,	13/8/16
3274	,,	HILL, C. V.	,, ,,	6/8/16
5037	Cpl.	SANSUM, A. H.	,, ,,	14/8/16
2323	Pte.	DEVENEY, P.	,, ,,	6/8/16
2474	,,	SMITH, R. S.	,, ,,	,,
3033	,,	DUNCAN, R. G.	,, ,,	12/8/16
3713	,,	KEAYS, A. C.	,, ,,	14/8/16
4004	,,	STURTRIDGE, G.	,, ,,	,,
3709	,,	KAY, J. F.	,, ,,	13/8/16
4348	,,	TILBEE, G. S.	,, ,,	,,
3997	,,	SMETHURST, J. H.	,, ,,	,,
4677	,,	MCKAY, A. A.	,, ,,	,,
2793	,,	DONOVAN, W. C.	,, ,,	,,
1746	,,	TWIGDEN, T. J.	,, ,,	14/8/16
1679	,,	BLENCOWE, A. H.	Died of Wounds	1/9/16
2630	Cpl.	MCLEOD, D. A.	,, ,,	2/9/16
4051	Pte.	WATKINS, A. E.	,, ,,	7/9/16
3140	,,	MATTHEWS, J. W.	Killed in Action	31/8/16
4370	,,	GORMAN, F.	,, ,,	7/8/16
3252	,,	DENNIS, A.	,, ,,	,,
2439	,,	WHITBREAD, L. J.	Died of Wounds	6/9/16
1765	,,	MANHIRE, H. R.	Killed in Action	6/8/16
5076	,,	COUSENS, F. E.	Died of Wounds	7/8/16
3051	,,	GILMORE, J.	,, ,,	1/9/16
1676	,,	BENSLEY, R. G.	,, ,,	16/9/16
4693	,,	ROSS, J. R.	Killed in Action	2/9/16
4132	,,	BRADEY, A. J.	,, ,,	,,
5065	,,	BELL, C. B.	,, ,,	,,
4565	,,	BANKS, S. A. G.	,, ,,	,,
4959	,,	WILLINGTON, S. W.	,, ,,	31/8/16
4872	,,	MILLS, J. G.	,, ,,	,,
1764	,,	MACKIE, J.	,, ,,	1/10/16
1838	,,	VERROALL, R.	,, ,,	,,
4689	,,	PATTISON, H. J. D.	,, ,,	30/9/16
4835	,,	JACKSON, P.	Died of Wounds	2/11/16
1745	,,	TRIPNEY, G. H.	Killed in Action	16/10/16

Reg'tl. No.	Rank	Name	Nature of Casualty	Date
1729	Pte.	SEARLE, J. P.	Killed in Action	16/10/16
1718	,,	PENTON, E. G.	,, ,,	15/10/16
3741	,,	OATEY, J. M.	,, ,,	,,
1659	,,	EVANS, E.	,, ,,	,,
121	,,	SCOTT, F. W.	,, ,,	,,
—	Lieut.	PHILIPPSON, C. L.	Died of Wounds	17/11/16
1798	Pte.	OUGDEN, F. L.	,, ,,	8/8/16
4102	,,	VINCE, A. E.	,, ,,	9/8/16
1714	,,	EDWARDS, P.	,, ,,	11/18/16
3119	,,	HOWLETT, P.	,, ,,	8/8/16
1777	R.S.M.	BENPORATH, F. H.	,, ,,	16/8/16
4652	Pte.	MINTY, E. J.	,, ,,	9/8/16
3065	,,	HUTCHINS, W. H.	Killed in Action	7/8/16
—	Lieut.	GUNNER, H.	,, ,,	30/9/16
1861	Pte.	BENNETT, J. P. A.	Died of Wounds	7/8/16
2789	,,	COX, J. P.	,, ,,	3/10/16
4834	,,	JONES, W.	,, ,,	2/10/16
2772	,,	SHORT, C. E.	,, ,,	1/10/16
3119	Sgt.	PRICE, A.	,, ,,	6/10/16
4780	Cpl.	CRAIG, J. B.	,, ,,	17/11/16
4811	Pte.	FLANAGAN, L.	,, ,,	2/11/16
1630	,,	BIGNELL, A.	Died of Illness	28/11/16
4541	L. Cpl.	GILBERT, R. W.	Died of Wounds	21/11/16
3003	Pte.	BEDFORD, T.	,, ,,	,,
4133	,,	BRADLEY, A. L.	,, ,,	14/11/16
4742	,,	ANDERSON, M.	Killed in Action	20/11/16
996	,,	CASTON, H.	,, ,,	23/11/16
2591	,,	STEVENS, W. H.	,, ,,	21/11/16
29	,,	COPELAND, J.	,, ,,	23/11/16
1712	,,	OLIVER, A. I.	,, ,,	20/11/16
5034	,,	HILL, B. T.	,, ,,	23/11/16
3658	,,	WOODLEY, S.	,, ,,	26/11/16
2382	,,	PARNELL, R. H.	,, ,,	,,
4428	,,	VAWDREY, T. F.	,, ,,	,,
3856	,,	BISHOP, W. J.	Died of Illness	9/12/16
2636	,,	JACKSON, J.	Died of Wounds	9/1/17
2366	,,	SHARP, H.	Died of Injuries	14/1/17
1669	,,	ASH, H. O.	Died of Wounds	22/1/17
4733	Sgt.	FERRIE, J.	,, ,,	24/1/17
2037	Pte.	YOUNG, H. M.	Killed in Action	8/1/17
4740	L. Cpl.	SMITH, R. V.	,, ,,	7/1/17
2003	Pte.	WEBB, W. B.	,, ,,	8/1/17
2470	,,	NELSON, O. H.	,, ,,	7/1/17
1713	,,	ORAM, J.	,, ,,	12/1/17
2420	,,	TALL, G. W.	,, ,,	,,
4144	,,	FINEY, H.	,, ,,	,,
1267	Sgt.	FOSTER, G.	,, ,,	15/1/17
2655	Pte.	EDMONDS, N. F.	Died of Illness	6/2/17
1733	,,	SMITH C	,, ,,	17/2/17

Reg'tl. No.	Rank and Name.		Nature of Casualty.	Date.
2683	Pte.	HEGARTY, J.	Died of Illness	22/2/17
1633	,,	BLIGHT, J. H.	Died of Wounds	27/2/17
1728	,,	SAWTELL, A. E.	,, ,,	2/3/17
2028	,,	MACKAY, H. G.	Died of Illness	3/3/17
5702	,,	GALL, J.	,, ,,	5/3/17
2374	,,	WILKINSON, C. P.	Killed in Action	20/2/17
1997	,,	TURLEY, G. C.	Died of Wounds	8/3/17
3989	,,	ROWLAND, C. J.	Killed in Action	10/4/17
200	L. Cpl.	BEECHEY, H. R.	,, ,,	10/4/17
—	Lieut.	WATSON, H. H.	,, ,,	11/4/17
5701	Pte.	FRANCIS, R. A.	,, ,,	8/4/17
2884	Cpl.	FLINT, G.	,, ,,	9/4/17
5072	Pte.	CUMMINGS, M. H.	,, ,,	,,
1580	Sgt.	ANDERSON, H. G.	,, ,,	11/4/17
1168	Pte.	ALLEN, H.	,, ,,	,,
1751	,,	WAY, M. L.	Died of Gas P'son'g	,,
2628	,,	HOLBERT, R. L.	Died of Wounds	12/4/17
—	Major	LEANE, B. B.	,, ,,	10/4/17
1931	Pte.	HAY, W. M.	,, ,,	24/4/17
—	Lieut.	WATSON, W.	,, ,,	28/4/17
4128	Pte.	BALD, A. H.	,, ,,	16/4/17
2057	,,	KELLY, L. A.	Killed in Action	11/4/17
3012	L. Cpl.	HUTTON, E. N.	,, ,,	,,
1919	Pte.	GALLAGHER, A. W.	,, ,,	,,
2424	,,	HOBBS, H. H.	,, ,,	,,
2296a	,,	BALDWIN, A. A.	,, ,,	,,
3228	L. Cpl.	BURN, R. W.	,, ,,	,,
3729	Pte.	MIATKE, F. A.	,, ,,	,,
1709	,,	MCLELLAN, J. H.	,, ,,	,,
3724	,,	MASTERS, R.	,, ,,	,,
—	Capt.	LEANE, A.	,, ,,	,,
2125	,,	BARRETT, R. H. E.	,, ,,	,,
1879	,,	BATES, B. S.	,, ,,	,,
—	2nd Lt.	HAMMOND, H. J.	,, ,,	,,
2983	Pte.	SIMS, F. G.	,, ,,	,,
2673	,,	HEALEY, J. S.	,, ,,	,,
2650	,,	DALZIELL, E.	,, ,,	,,
2649	,,	DOYLE, W.	,, ,,	,,
4794	,,	DAVIES, H. G.	,, ,,	,,
2665	,,	GIBSON, G. W.	,, ,,	,,
5040	L. Cpl.	JOHNSON, J. F.	,, ,,	,,
2698	Pte.	LOUDEN, H. G. A.	,, ,,	,,
2720b	,,	MARCH, D. G.	,, ,,	,,
2714	,,	MARSHALL, W. J.	,, ,,	,,
2706	,,	MCCABE, J.	,, ,,	,,
2705	,,	MCKINNON, A.	,, ,,	,,
2712	,,	MESNEY, V. W.	,, ,,	,,
16	Sgt.	FOSTER, A. B.	,, ,,	,,
4758	Pte.	BUSWELL, G. E.	,, ,,	,,

"OUR DEAD."

Reg'tl. No.	Rank and Name.		Nature of Casualty.	Date.
2751	Pte.	TRELOAR, P. C.	Killed in Action	11/4/17
4347	L. Cpl.	TICKLIE, A. T.	,, ,,	,,
1723	,,	GAMLEN, A. S.	,, ,,	,,
5111a	Pte.	HICKEY, J.	,, ,,	,,
1921	,,	GEBHARDT, E. G. L.	,, ,,	,,
4280	,,	GOODMAN, F. J.	,, ,,	,,
—	2nd Lt.	BLASKETT, W. G.	,, ,,	,,
—	,,	JONES, S. E.	,, ,,	,,
4890	Pte.	TOBIN, W. J.	Died of Wounds	15/1/17
1731	,,	SHILLABEER, A. A.	Killed in Action	11/4/17
2368	L. Cpl.	RICHARDS, R. M. T.	,, ,,	,,
3122	Pte.	DONALD, W.	,, ,,	,,
1989	,,	SIVIOUR, N. R.	,, ,,	,,
2253	L. Cpl.	THOMAS, W. H.	,, ,,	,,
1395	Cpl.	WHITE, F. O.	,, ,,	,,
2263	Pte.	WHEELER, T. L.	,, ,,	,,
2214	,,	NEVILLE, M. A.	,, ,,	,,
4650	Cpl.	MILLAR, A. B.	,, ,,	,,
2247	Pte.	SMITH, G.	,, ,,	16/4/17
511	,,	LAWLOR, J.	,, ,,	11/4/17
4632	,,	JECKS, A. C.	,, ,,	,,
4683	,,	ONSLOW, E.	,, ,,	,,
5411	,,	McLEAN, K.	,, ,,	,,
3990	,,	RUSSELL, G. A.	,, ,,	,,
5085	,,	DONOVAN, C.	,, ,,	,,
2151	,,	DURDIN, W. J.	,, ,,	,,
2475	,,	FULWOOD, W. D.	,, ,,	,,
2149	,,	DRENNAN, D. McN.	,, ,,	,,
1889	,,	BROOKS, H. P.	Died of Wounds	,,
2863	,,	BLENCOWE, S. F.	,, ,,	,,
1900	,,	CORNISH, H. G.	,, ,,	,,
4183	,,	SCANTLEBURY, H. E.	,, ,,	12/4/17
2643	,,	CHANTLER, C. G.	,, ,,	11/4/17
5113	L. Cpl.	HAMILL, A. C.	,, ,,	14/4/17
2431	,,	HOPSON, W. H.	,, ,,	12/4/17
1689	Pte.	LAWRIE, N. H.	,, ,,	13/5/17
4950	,,	BALDRY, F. O.	,, ,,	11/4/17
2459	,,	MYERS, J. E.	Killed in Action	,,
4451	Cpl.	WACHMAN, R.	,, ,,	,,
26 9	P.e.	BRUCE, A. E.	,, ,,	,,
1998a	L. Cpl.	CROWE, R. C.	,, ,,	,,
5679	,,	COOPER, S. R.	,, ,,	,,
2399	Pte.	COOMBS, N.	,, ,,	,,
2123a	,,	BARBER, J. R.	,, ,,	,,
421	,,	ANDERSON, K. C.	,, ,,	,,
2489	,,	SMITH, A.	,, ,,	,,
2492	,,	SHUKARD, W. G.	,, ,,	,,
2243	,,	SHEPHERD, D. R.	,, ,,	,,
1976	,,	ROBERTS, H. E.	,, ,,	,,

Reg'tl. No.	Rank and Name.		Nature of Casualty.	Date.
1724	Pte.	RIGBY, J. W.	Killed in Action	11/4/17
5849	,,	PARSONS, W. G.	,, ,,	,,
2470	,,	PATTERSON, O. N.	,, ,,	,,
3740	,,	NOY, E. H.	,, ,,	,,
588	,,	NOY, L. C.	,, ,,	,,
1888	,,	BROOKS, C.	,, ,,	,,
1934	,,	HOLLAND, H. J.	,, ,,	,,
2276	,,	GREGORY, A.	,, ,,	,,
4147	,,	GLOVER, H.	,, ,,	,,
1911	,,	EVANS, C. R.	,, ,,	,,
2299	,,	DOLAN, M.	,, ,,	,,
1905	L. Cpl.	DEANE, J. S.	,, ,,	,,
5680	Pte.	CUNDY, W. D.	,, ,,	,,
2314	,,	COOMBS, K.	,, ,,	,,
2138	,,	CHRISTIAN, A. J.	,, ,,	,,
2142a	,,	COOMBS, J. J.	,, ,,	,,
2332	,,	COLEBATCH, H. E.	,, ,,	,,
2461	,,	CLEARY, A. H.	,, ,,	,,
1880	,,	BATES, G. T.	,, ,,	,,
1650	,,	CLAPP, J.	,, ,,	,,
518	,,	MOUNCE, C. A.	,, ,,	,,
1937	,,	IRELAND, W. J.	,, ,,	,,
4163	,,	LOVE, S. E.	,, ,,	,,
1950	,,	LeBRUN, W. H.	,, ,,	,,
1169	L. Cpl.	HARVEY, L. W.	,, ,,	,,
2151a	Sgt.	HARRIS, I.	,, ,,	,,
5711	Pte.	HORNE, A. V.	,, ,,	,,
2510	,,	WRIGHT, D. L.	,, ,,	,,
2453a	,,	WARD, A.	,, ,,	,,
935a	,,	MAHONEY, C.	,, ,,	,,
2033a	L. Cpl.	WRIGHT, E. J.	,, ,,	,,
2012	Pte.	WOOLRIDGE, S. J. C. G.	,, ,,	,,
2838b	L. Cpl.	WILLIAMS, G. S.	,, ,,	,,
2507	Pte.	WIESE, R. G. W.	,, ,,	,,
5728	,,	MAYELL, E. J.	,, ,,	,,
1385	Cpl.	WARREN, U. G.	,, ,,	,,
2259	Pte.	VINEY, E. G.	,, ,,	,,
2499	,,	TURNER, C. C.	,, ,,	,,
3016	,,	BURLACE, C. C.	,, ,,	,,
3087b	Cpl.	LAHEY, J. H.	,, ,,	,,
3117	Pte.	PAGE, A. J.	,, ,,	,,
3111	Cpl.	NICHOLSON, J. W.	,, ,,	,,
3041	Pte.	EVANS, R. H.	,, ,,	,,
3063	L. Sgt.	COOPER, J. C.	,, ,,	,,
129	Pte.	HEATH, H.	Died of Wounds	3/6/17
2173	,,	HARRIS, V. C.	,, ,,	9/6/17
2275	,,	LAURIE, C. A.	Killed in Action	11/4/17
5130	,,	LLOYD, W.	Died of Wounds	8/6/17
—	Capt.	MAYERSBETH, J. W.	Killed in Action	12/6/17

"OUR DEAD."

Reg'tl. No.	Rank	Name	Nature of Casualty	Date
—	Lieut.	CODDINGTON-FORSYTH, G.P.	Killed in Action	12/6/17
1799	Pte.	PEREIRA, E. M.	,, ,,	8/6/17
1641	,,	CALLARD, J. E.	,, ,,	,,
2350	L. Cpl.	KILMARTIN, F. T. J.	,, ,,	,,
3289	Pte.	McCANN, J.	,, ,,	,,
5666	,,	BUSBRIDGE, R. J.	,, ,,	9/6/17
3256	,,	EARLE, F. H.	,, ,,	,,
1764	,,	RITTMAN, E. M. A.	,, ,,	,,
2278	,,	JONAS, A. R. B.	,, ,,	,,
3744	,,	PAREH, M. M.	,, ,,	,,
2246	,,	SMITH, G.	,, ,,	8/6/17
1902	,,	CRITCHLEY, M. F.	,, ,,	12/6/17
2205	,,	MEGAW, S. G.	,, ,,	,,
1679	,,	JAMES, W.	,, ,,	11/4/17
2918	Sgt.	O'BRIEN, M. P.	,, ,,	11/6/17
2753	Pte.	TOMLINSON, J. D.	,, ,,	9/6/17
2935	,,	KINNANE, T.	,, ,,	11/6/17
3017	L. Cpl.	JOHNSON, C. T.	,, ,,	9/6/17
2901	Pte.	EDBROOKE, F. C.	,, ,,	,,
2048	Cpl.	TURNER, P. T.	,, ,,	12/6/17
2875	Pte.	BADNALL, C. B.	,, ,,	2/6/17
1884	,,	BIRD, H.	Died of Wounds	14/4/17
2332a	,,	FRASER, F.	Died of Illness	23/5/17
4842	,,	KIRKPATRICK, R. L.	Died of Wounds	8/7/17
2279a	,,	KIRWAN, R. J.	,, ,,	4/7/17
1998	,,	TURNER, H. H.	,, ,,	16/4/17
3236	,,	WALLACE, W. C.	,, ,,	11/7/17
2882	,,	BLECHYNDEN, L. T.	,, ,,	1/7/17
2882	,,	ELSHAW, J. W. B.	,, ,,	,,
2474	,,	RYAN, E. J.	Killed in Action	10/7/17
1913	,,	FARMER, H.	,, ,,	,,
2932	,,	KEYTE, C. C.	,, ,,	,,
3727	Cpl.	MARSHALL, F. S.	Died of Wounds	13/4/17
3987	T. Sgt.	ROBINSON, C. W.	,, ,,	15/4/17
2159	Pte.	GARDNER, W. H.	,, ,,	13/4/17
2163a	,,	GRANT, A. A.	,, ,,	,,
1680	,,	JEFFS, C.	,, ,,	,,
2950	,,	McKILLOP, D.	Killed in Action	15/7/17
2956	,,	MOCATTI, V. J.	,, ,,	,,
2464	,,	MARRINER, R. F.	Died of Wounds	18/7/17
6601	,,	MUTRIE, H.	,, ,,	18/8/17
2195	,,	LEVETT, A. R.	Died other causes	13/4/17
3012a	,,	BASS, J.	Killed in Action	9/8/17
—	Major	HOWDEN, M. C.	Died of Wounds	5/7/17
2235	Pte.	ROBINSON, F. G.	,, ,,	27/8/17
4503	,,	BARRY, T.	Killed in Action	10/8/17
4504	,,	BURROWS, R.	,, ,,	,,
4625	,,	GORDON, D.	,, ,,	,,
1726	L. Cpl.	ROPER, L. E. T.	,, ,,	,,

Reg'tl. No.		Rank and Name.	Nature of Casualty.	Date.
3462	Pte.	Tuck, F. C. C.	Killed in Action	10/8/17
2680a	,,	Hocking, J. H.	,, ,,	8/8/17
2648	,,	Devon, R.	,, ,,	9/8/17
724	,,	O'Neill, E.	,, ,,	,,
990	,,	Snaden, G. J.	,, ,,	,,
2176	,,	Hemsley, C. A.	Died of Wounds	
2218	,,	O'Neil, D. J.	,, ,,	6/5/17
3389	,,	Fenwick, W. E.	,, ,,	15/8/17
2034	,,	Whittaker, L. B.	Killed in Action	11/8/17
2716	,,	Martin, G. T.	Died of Wounds	15/8/17
2477a	,,	Tutt, A.	Killed in Action	11/4/17
2467a	L. Cpl.	O'Brien, J. D.	,, ,,	,,
1946	Pte.	Kilntworth, H. L.	,, ,,	,,
4684	,,	Oxman, A. W.	,, ,,	,,
5133	,,	Lowe, R.	,, ,,	,,
4948	,,	Hebenton, T.	,, ,,	,,
1938	,,	Speck, J. C.	,, ,,	,,
3044	L. Cpl.	Emmins, A. O.	,, ,,	,,
5847	Pte.	Nicholas, C. R.	Died other causes	8/8/17
3302	,,	Richards, R. M.	,, ,,	9/4/17
3044	,,	Bruce, W. R.	Died of Wounds	29/9/17
3218	,,	Stokes, C. J.	,, ,,	30/9/17
1812	,,	Rowe, W.	,, ,,	28/9/17
2610	,,	Drever, F. N.	,, ,,	,,
5078	,,	Collier, G.	Killed in Action	11/4/17
4803	,,	Ellement, V. E.	Died of Wounds	14/10/17
2738	,,	Robb, J. G.	,, ,,	13/10/17
4171	Sgt.	McArthur, C. N.	Killed in Action	1/10/17
2439	Cpl.	Jeffery, A.	,, ,,	29/9/17
3422	Pte.	Dunstan, O. P.	,, ,,	,,
2452	,,	Martin, J. T.	Died of Wounds	1/10/17
—	Lieut.	Murray, E. A. M.	Killed in Action	12/10/17
—	,,	Ridley, H. Q.	,, ,,	11/10/17
3464	Pte.	Wade, R. V.	Died of Wounds	13/10/17
1868	Cpl.	Harvey, E.	,, ,,	18/10/17
—	Lieut.	Grinlington, D.	,, ,,	17/10/17
3165	Pte.	Henry, J. W.	,, ,,	14/10/17
2410	,,	Edwards, C.	,, ,,	22/10/17
3718	L. Sgt.	Lindner, L. W.	,, ,,	,,
4810	Pte.	Flynn, T. J.	Died other causes	9/4/17
1678	,,	Irwin, B. J.	Died of Wounds	17/10/17
2881	,,	Blooman, H.	,, ,,	18/10/17
4332	,,	Denham, F. A.	,, ,,	12/10/17
2194	,,	Lethbridge, E. M.	Killed in Action	11/10/17
3380	Pte.	Cameron, E. A.	,, ,,	12/10/17
3250	,,	Deardon, F.	,, ,,	,,
4700	,,	Dorling, A. R. G.	,, ,,	,,
2152	Sgt.	Ellery, C. F. S.	,, ,,	,,
3695	Pte.	Feely, E. J.	,, ,,	,,

"OUR DEAD."

Reg'tl. No.		Rank and Name.	Nature of Casualty.	Date.
3388	Pte.	FERGUSON, C.	Killed in Action	12/10/17
2532	,,	FERGUSON, R. H.	,, ,,	,,
5700	,,	FRANCIS, J. B.	,, ,,	,,
1669	,,	GIBBS, W. A.	,, ,,	,,
2513	Cpl.	HASS, W. T.	,, ,,	,,
3157	Pte.	HUNTER, R. O.	,, ,,	,,
3249	,,	HOOPER, W. K.	,, ,,	,,
4627	,,	HILL, H. C.	,, ,,	,,
3029	,,	GRAHAM, F.	,, ,,	,,
2909	,,	GANT, G.	,, ,,	,,
3101	,,	DORAN, A. P.	,, ,,	,,
4571	,,	BROOKS, T.	,, ,,	,,
3104b	,,	BRITTAIN, W. W.	,, ,,	,,
438	L. Cpl.	BREUER, J. H.	,, ,,	,,
2627	,,	BOWES, J. B.	,, ,,	,,
3296	Pte.	O'REILLY, T.	,, ,,	,,
3368	,,	BOEHM, H. J.	,, ,,	,,
1828	,,	SWATKINS, C. H.	Died of Wounds	3/11/17
5729	,,	MAYTUM, E. N.	,, ,,	1/11/17
670	L. Cpl.	KIRK, A.	Killed in Action	12/10/17
2181	Pte.	HURCOMB, V. A. R.	,, ,,	,,
1693	,,	LONERGAN, J.	,, ,,	,,
2456	Cpl.	MUNT, H.	,, ,,	,,
4572	Pte.	O'CONNOR, J. B.	,, ,,	,,
3474	,,	McMUTRIE, H.	,, ,,	,,
1714	,,	PARKER, W. C.	,, ,,	,,
3486	,,	PAGE, H. K.	,, ,,	,,
2281	L. Cpl.	PEARCE, J.	,, ,,	,,
3303	Pte.	ROGERS, C. S.	,, ,,	,,
5329	Sgt.	ROBERTSON, W. G.	,, ,,	,,
2233	Cpl.	RINDER, G.	,, ,,	,,
2250	Pte.	STRATFORD, G.	,, ,,	,,
1391	,,	WICKER, A.	,, ,,	,,
2009	,,	WILLIAMS, W. H.	,, ,,	,,
1970	,,	PHILBEY, A. L.	,, ,,	,,
3043	L. Cpl.	JAMES, P. E.	,, ,,	,,
4868	Pte.	MALEY, R. H.	,, ,,	,,
3032	,,	LAWSON, J.	,, ,,	,,
4102	,,	OSBORN, W. A. J.	,, ,,	,,
2756	,,	THOMPSON, S. R.	,, ,,	,,
3217	,,	SHANKS, D.	,, ,,	,,
2860	,,	WRIGHTSON, A. H.	,, ,,	,,
1418	,,	HYRONS, J.	,, ,,	20/10/17
3417	,,	MARTIN, F. H.	,, ,,	,,
2629	,,	BARTER, R. D.	,, ,,	,,
2880	L. Cpl.	BACKSHALL, W. J.	,, ,,	,,
2414	Pte.	FRASER, G. A.	Died of Wounds	1/5/17
3000	,,	THOMPSON, W. J.	Died of Illness	24/11/17
3139	,,	COWAN, J.	Died of Wounds	,,

Reg'tl. No.	Rank and Name.		Nature of Casualty.	Date.
2016	Cpl.	Richards, A. S.	Died of Illness	1/12/17
2984	Pte.	Sims, F. A.	Killed in Action	11/4/17
3872	,,	Rigney, R. G.	Died of Wounds	16/10/17
3403	,,	Bentley, E.	Died of Illness	22/12/17
3465	,,	Wells, G.	Killed in Action	12/10/17
2524	,,	Hutchison, S. J.	Died of Wounds	21/10/17
2002	,,	Watson, J. R.	Killed in Action	11/4/17
2140	,,	Collaton, F. P.	,, ,,	12/10/17
5683	,,	Danford, C.	,, ,,	,,
1907	,,	Dyson, T. H.	,, ,,	,,
3386	,,	Edwards, D.	,, ,,	,,
3390	,,	Gilbert, S. J.	,, ,,	,,
3702	,,	Hayes, E. P.	,, ,,	,,
5839	,,	Hewish, H.	,, ,,	,,
2183	,,	Isaacson, W. E.	,, ,,	,,
2434a	,,	Johnston, W.	,, ,,	,,
1944	,,	Keneally, T. C.	,, ,,	,,
1688	,,	Lane, N. C.	,, ,,	,,
2024	Sgt.	Langsford, A. N.	,, ,,	,,
3720	Pte.	Lindsay, W. C. L.	,, ,,	,,
2872	,,	Allan, S. D.	,, ,,	,,
3026	,,	Allen, E.	,, ,,	,,
3114	,,	Applin, R. H.	,, ,,	,,
2633	,,	Boucher, A.	,, ,,	11/4/17
3254	,,	Bray, H. O.	,, ,,	12/10/17
3132	,,	Card, F. J.	,, ,,	,,
5032	,,	Carroll, A. E.	,, ,,	,,
4593	Sgt.	Davis, J. (Zimmer, J.)	,, ,,	,,
2613	,,	Daue, S.	,, ,,	,,
2191	Pte.	White, J. H.	,, ,,	,,
2036	,,	Williams, W.	,, ,,	,,
3012a	,,	Wood, C.	,, ,,	,,
3024	,,	Taylor, J.	,, ,,	,,
3235	,,	Watt, J. A.	,, ,,	,,
3007	,,	Westergaard, E.	,, ,,	,,
3240	,,	Whitehand, R. G.	,, ,,	,,
2704	,,	Quinlan, J. A. "M.M."	,, ,,	,,
1975	Cpl.	Roachock, T. J.	,, ,,	,,
4198	Pte.	Robinson, R. G. "M.M."	,, ,,	,,
2720	,,	Scriven, L. R.	,, ,,	,,
3610	,,	Souter, F. H.	,, ,,	,,
2252	A. Sgt.	Symonds, A. G.	,, ,,	,,
4181	C.S.M.	Russell, W. P.	,, ,,	,,
3353	,,	Clark, E. J.	,, ,,	,,
1660	,,	Eveson, T.	,, ,,	,,
3363	,,	Brooks, T. A.	,, ,,	,,
1815	Pte.	Rumbelow, F. H.	,, ,,	,,
3144	,,	Michie, J.	,, ,,	,,
1301	,,	Marshall T. E.	,, ..	,,

Reg'tl. No.	Rank	Rank and Name	Nature of Casualty	Date
1700	Pte.	MEAKINS, E. A.	Killed in Action	12/10/17
2132	,,	MOGG, B. S.	,, ,,	,,
1760	,,	WRIGHT, J. H. D.	Died of Wounds	5/10/17
3197	,,	POTTER, H. E.	Killed in Action	12/10/17
—	Lieut.	GUTHRIE, R. S.	,, ,,	,,
4330	,,	RUSSELL, W. A.	,, ,,	,,
2987	,,	SCARESBROOK, F. C.	,, ,,	,,
3224	,,	SELBY, S. V.	,, ,,	,,
3103	,,	SIMPSON, A. S.	,, ,,	,,
3222	,,	STUBBS-MILLS, E.	,, ,,	,,
2866	,,	FINN, F.	,, ,,	,,
2657	,,	FORBES, A. McD.	,, ,,	,,
2666	,,	CREAGG, J. R.	,, ,,	,,
2674	,,	HAEMER, W.	,, ,,	,,
5114	L. Cpl.	HARRIS, J. A.	,, ,,	,,
3166	Pte.	HENFRY, E. L. B.	,, ,,	,,
3159	,,	HODGINS, R.	,, ,,	,,
2711	,,	MOULDEN, W.	,, ,,	,,
2961	,,	NEWPORT, C. V.	,, ,,	,,
2963	,,	NIXON, C. E.	,, ,,	,,
2713	,,	ROSS, D.	Died of Wounds	5/4/17
2423	,,	THULBORN, F. P.	,, ,,	,,
4785	,,	COLLINS, L. F.	Died of Illness	26/1/18
2701	,,	LILLY, F.	Killed in Action	27/3/18
2220	,,	O'NEILL, W. P., "M.M."	Died of Wounds	8/4/18
3925	,,	BOROWSKI, L. P.	Killed in Action	28/3/18
—	Lieut.	MAYNARD, H. H., "M.M."	,, ,,	5/4/18
1968	Sgt.	BARBER, A. A., "M.M."	,, ,,	28/3/18
3357	Pte.	DORE, G. H.	,, ,,	,,
1670	,,	GLASSENBURY, F. G.	,, ,,	,,
2967	,,	OMA, N.	,, ,,	5/4/18
1690a	,,	CEANDLER, S. H.	,, ,,	,,
2272	,,	CHELLEW, B. E.	,, ,,	3/4/18
2302	L. Cpl.	SCOTT, J.	,, ,,	5/4/18
2015	Sgt.	MACLOY, M. H.	,, ,,	,,
563	,,	O'SULLIVAN, P.	,, ,,	,,
2122	,,	BAKER, W. R.	,, ,,	,,
4750	,,	BLACKMAN, E.	,, ,,	,,
2504	Pte.	TUDOR, S. R.	,, ,,	,,
3327	Cpl.	WHITAKER, T. W.	,, ,,	,,
2988	,,	SMALL, W. C., "M.M."	,, ,,	,,
2763	L. Cpl.	DONALDSON, J. A.	,, ,,	,,
3020a	,,	NOLAN, A. P.	,, ,,	,,
1876	,,	O'BRIEN, W. A.	,, ,,	,,
3751	C.Q.M.S.	ROCHOW, F. A.	,, ,,	,,
3475	Pte.	McCULLOUGH, R. A.	,, ,,	28/3/18
2463a	,,	McDONALD, A. A.	,, ,,	,,
4594	,,	DEDMAN, G.	,, ,,	3/4/18
3117a	,,	HOWSON, R. R.	,, ,,	,,

Reg'tl. No.	Rank and Name.		Nature of Casualty.	Date.
4861	Pte.	McNee, W.	Killed in Action	27/3/18
3198	,,	Prince, A.	,, ,,	28/3/18
2858	L. Cpl.	Mackenzie, A. C.	,, ,,	5/4/18
2857	Pte.	McCombe, M. S.	,, ,,	,,
2702	,,	McGowan, T.	,, ,,	,,
3637	,,	Dobson, A. C.	,, ,,	14/2/18
—	Lieut.	Whittle, J.	,, ,,	29/3/18
—	Capt.	Elliott, T. H.	,, ,,	28/3/18
4379	Pte.	Hemming, J. J.	Died of Wounds	,,
3672	,,	Leishman, J. F. T.	,, ,,	31/3/18
1773	,,	Moore, F. A.	,, ,,	28/3/18
2405	,,	Scott, E. A.	,, ,,	30/3/18
2896	,,	Cousins, V. D.	Died other causes	9/2/18
4872	,,	White, C. J.	Died of Wounds	5/4/18
3377	,,	Church, A. E.	Killed in Action	27/3/18
1704	,,	Davies, W. A.	Died of Wounds	4/4/18
2137	,,	Chappel, C. L.	,, ,,	28/4/18
3698	,,	Rogers, A. C.	,, ,,	4/5/18
—	Lieut.	Ferguson, A. S.	Killed in Action	3/5/18
—	,,	Garland, H. G., "D.C.M."	,, ,,	,,
3662	Pte.	Johnson, G.	Died of Wounds	,,
—	Capt.	Cumming, D.G.C. "M.C."	Killed in Action	,,
—	Lieut.	Luetchford, D.F., "M.M."	,, ,,	,,
2231	Pte.	Reid, A. B.	Died of Wounds	4/5/18
2752	,,	Trotter, J. A.	,, ,,	,,
3109	,,	McAllan, W.	Killed in Action	27/4/18
2152	,,	Amey, T. J.	,, ,,	3/5/18
6762	A. Sgt.	Barnard, S. H.	,, ,,	,,
1520	Pte.	Brennan, J.	,, ,,	,,
1640a	,,	Brown, E. F., "M.M."	,, ,,	,,
3865	,,	Kennedy, W.	,, ,,	,,
3419	,,	Millar, R. G.	,, ,,	,,
6126	,,	Nicholls, J. W.	,, ,,	,,
4620	,,	Wilson, E. J.	,, ,,	,,
5045	,,	Kelly, N. W.	,, ,,	,,
4306	,,	Burrington, H. F.	,, ,,	,,
4349	,,	James, O.	,, ,,	,,
4353	,,	Kay, C. W.	,, ,,	,,
2936	,,	Kendall, D. G.	,, ,,	,,
2930	,,	Smith, J.	,, ,,	,,
2409	,,	Evans, H. E.	Died of Wounds	15/5/18
6881	,,	Roberts, G. E.	,, ,,	12/5/18
1887	,,	Brogan, J.	,, ,,	3/5/18
6851	,,	Miller, R. R.	,, ,,	,,
6896	,,	Smallacombe, G. P.	,, ,,	,,
3919	,,	Thompson, G. T.	,, ,,	,,
5864	,,	Wilks, M. T.	,, ,,	,,
2679	,,	Hinxman, H.	Killed in Action	10/5/18
4342	,,	Holbrook, T. C.	Died of Wounds	19/5/18

Reg'tl. No.		Rank and Name.	Nature of Casualty.	Date.
3667	Pte.	KEEFE, E.	Killed in Action	12/5/18
4776	,,	CONNAUGHTON, W. J.,'M.M'	,, ,,	14/5/18
3861	,,	CATTERMOLE, F. J.	Died of Illness	14/6/18
4837	,,	PACKER, J. H.	Killed in Action	3/5/18
3402	,,	HOSKINS, W.	Died of Wounds	23/4/18
1139	,,	CONNELL, J.	,, ,,	25/6/18
3628	,,	COOMBE, W. J.	,, ,,	30/6/18
2169	,,	GREIG, W. R.	,, ,,	26/6/18
6883	,,	SELWAY, G.	,, ,,	25/6/18
3114	,,	HANNAN, L. V.	,, ,,	29/6/18
3701	,,	SAMPSON, J.	Killed in Action	23/6/18
3317	,,	TAYLOR, G. F.	,, ,,	24/6/18
6819	,,	GORE, B.	Died of Wounds	23/6/18
4163	,,	LEE, R. E.	Killed in Action	8/7/18
3939a	,,	HERGSTROM, C. T.	,, ,,	3/7/13
3411	,,	KENNEDY, A. C.	,, ,,	29/6/13
1781	,,	McDONALD, H. R.	,, ,,	3/7/13
2416	,,	STANLEY, W.	,, ,,	28/6/13
6904	,,	VENABLES, R. D.	,, ,,	29/6/13
1854	Cpl.	WILLIS, J.	Died of Illness	11/7/18
5046	Pte.	ANNANDALE, J. W.	,, ,,	29/6/18
4567	Sgt.	BEATON, E., " M.M."	,, ,,	1/7/18
3221	Pte.	SOUTER, J. McG.	,, ,,	6/4/18
3449	,,	HANSBERRY, J. M.	Died of Wounds	15/7/18
4888	,,	LAUREN, K. W. W.	,, ,,	12/7/18
4300a	,,	BULL, F.	,, ,,	11/7/18
3839	,,	FOREMAN, C. W. E.	Killed in Action	8/7/18
6798	,,	CLASOHM, S. E.	Died of Wounds	12/7/18
4772	,,	CALHOUN, W.	Killed in Action	6/7/18
6807	,,	DRUMMOND, R. I.	,, ,,	3/5/18
6913	,,	HILL, A. J.	,, ,,	,,
3945	,,	HUTCHINSON, F. M.	,, ,,	,,
2352	T. Cpl.	INGLIS, E. C.	,, ,,	,,
3451	L. Cpl.	JOSEPH, P. H. M.	,, ,,	,,
1697	Pte.	MALLYON, A. K.	,, ,,	,,
2615r	,,	QUINN, C. E. L.	,, ,,	,,
4870	,,	WILLIAMS, F. G.	,, ,,	,,
5064b	,,	BOTTEN, G.	,, ,,	,,
2654	,,	ELMS, H.	,, ,,	,,
3162	,,	HAYDOCK, F.	,, ,,	,,
3647	,,	GENGE, J. W.	Died of Wounds	2/8/18
2684	,,	HITCHCOCK, H.	Killed in Action	3/5/18
4394	,,	TOUGH, A.	,, ,,	,,
6524	,,	HARRIS, C. F.	Died of Wounds	8/8/18
—	2nd Lt.	O'NEILL, J. G.	Killed in Action	,,
1947a	Cpl.	KIRKBRIGHT, E.	Died of Wounds	9/8/18
4443a	Pte.	O'BRIEN, J.	,, ,,	,,
1611a	Sgt.	DICKSON, W. D.,"D.C.M."	,, ,,	,,
3126	Cpl.	REYCRAFT, W.	,, ,,	,,

Reg'tl. No.	Rank	and Name.	Nature of Casualty.	Date.
1642	Cpl.	CARR, W. H.	Died of Illness	20/8/18
6919	Pte.	BARBERY, N.	Died of Wounds	22/8/18
2647	,,	CAPORN, P.	Killed in Action	8/8/18
3212	,,	RICKEY, E. E.	,, ,,	,,
4435	,,	WHARTON, W. M., "M.M."	Died of Wounds	21/8/18
4256	,,	CONROY, J. W.	,, ,,	8/8/18
1638	,,	BRICE, E. C.	Killed in Action	5/8/18
2189	,,	KENTISH, R. S.	,, ,,	8/8/18
4169	,,	MASON, C. W.	,, ,,	,,
2219	,,	O'NEILL, P.	,, ,,	,,
4864	,,	THOMPSON, J.	,, ,,	,,
2254	,,	TIDMARSH, C. E.	,, ,,	,,
3266	,,	CLARK, A.	,, ,,	,,
4354	,,	KENT, E. S.	,, ,,	,,
3180	Cpl.	MOLONEY, J.	,, ,,	,,
1703	,,	MOIR, P.	Died of Illness	31/10/18
3040	,,	TALBOT, H. A., "M.M."	Killed in Action	8/8/18
4364	Pte.	YOUNG, A. G.	,, ,,	,,
2477b	Sgt.	RUNDLE, L. L.	Died of Wounds	23/8/18
3107	Pte.	FARRELL, J.	Killed in Action	3/5/18
4437	,,	GRIMSTER, F. C.	,, ,,	,,
—	Lieut.	WHITE, A. D.	Died of Wounds	18/9/18
2148	Cpl.	DOSWELL, F. J.	,, ,,	24/9/18
3862	Pte.	JENKINS, S. J.	,, ,,	18/9/18
3720	,,	THOMPSON, C. J.	,, ,,	21/9/18
2747	Cpl.	STEWART, H.	,, ,,	18/9/18
6792	Pte.	BROWNE, J. H.	Killed in Action	,,
6827	,,	HELIER, W.	,, ,,	,,
6832	,,	ILLMAN, H. F.	,, ,,	,,
3278	Cpl.	LAPTHORNE, T. F.	,, ,,	,,
2159	Pte.	LUNT, N.	,, ,,	20/9/18
1614	Sgt.	SMITH, J. W.	,, ,,	18/9/18
3413	Pte.	LAYCOCK, F. O.	Died of Wounds	23/8/18
—	Lieut.	SHELDON, W. C.	,, ,,	4/10/18
2940	Pte.	LIND, C.	Killed in Action	18/9/18
2927	,,	SAMPFORD, C. R.	,, ,,	,,
1178	,,	STANGER, W. W.	,, ,,	,,
4352	,,	VALLI, B.	,, ,,	,,
1951	L. Cpl.	LEO, J. J.	Died of Wounds	,,
6784	Pte.	BARNES, J. T.	Died other causes	10/10/18
4291	,,	CLARK, A. B.	Killed in Action	18/9/18
3446	,,	BARDON, G.	Died other causes	13/10/18
4306	,,	CUSACK, W.	,, ,,	9/10/18
4765	,,	BENNETT, F. N.	Killed in Action	5/4/18
1658	,,	DRUMMOND, H. M.	,, ,,	,,
2435a	L. Cpl.	JAMES, A. M.	,, ,,	,,
2427	Pte.	TOTHILL, H. J.	,, ,,	,,
3772	,,	WHITEFORD, J. W.	,, ,,	6/4/18
3812	,,	BORGMEYER, A. J.	Died other causes	17/10/18

"OUR DEAD."

Reg'tl. No.	Rank and Name.		Nature of Casualty.	Date.
3122	Pte.	BISHOP, H. H.	Killed in Action	5/4/18
2944	,,	MUNDY, W. H.	,, ,,	,,
4448	Cpl.	ROGERS, D. O.	,, ,,	6/4/18
2859	Sgt.	O'NEIL, G. D.	,, ,,	20/9/18
3195	Pte.	PITT, C. L.	Accidentally Killed	3/10/18
2311	,,	COLLINS, H. G.	Died of Illness	30/10/18
5080	,,	DUGGAN, P. C.	Died of Injuries	,,
2401a	,,	CRABB, H. A. F.	,, ,,	,,
3857	,,	HOLLAMBY, D. E.	Died of Illness	12/12/18
3416	,,	MARTIN, A. H.	,, ,,	11/12/18
—	Lieut.	WARD, L. N., "M.C."	Killed in Action	19/9/18
2370a	L. Cpl.	UNWIN, W.	Died of Wounds	29/3/19
945	,,	TONKIN, J. J.	Died of Illness	29/12/18
3022	,,	CLIFF, T.	,, ,,	9/1/19
2678	,,	HORE, F. M.	,, ,,	31/12/18
1694	,,	LUCAS, B. O.	,, ,,	6/2/19
4441	,,	FERGUSON, E. C.	,, ,,	,,
2722	Pte.	NORTHEY, H. H.	,, ,,	15/2/19
1740	,,	SUHARD, K. R. J.	,, ,,	13/2/19
2885	,,	BROWNE, W. T.	,, ,,	15/2/19
3910	,,	CONDON, T. R.	,, ,,	18/3/19
6799	,,	CARLSON, C.	Died other causes	8/4/19
1485	,,	STAFFORD, P. G.	,, ,,	26/2/19
2478	,,	WAANDERS, W. R.	,, ,,	20/5/19

MAY THEY REST IN PEACE.

APPENDIX III.

Victoria Cross :—Woods, Pte. James P.

C.M.G. :—Leane, Lt. Col. R. L.

D.S.O. :—Anderson, Capt. A. M. ; Leane; Lt.-Col. R. L. (with bar) ; Perry, Lt.-Col. S. L.

M.C. :—Anderson, Capt. F. ; Bonython, Lieut. G. ; Burnett, Lieut. H. J. ; Corr, Lieut. W. B. ; Challen, Lieut. L. G. R. ; Collins, Capt. A. (attached) ; Dennis, Lieut. E. J. ; Fairley, Lieut. T. C. ; Hammond, Capt. T. R. ; Imlay, Lieut. N. G. ; Leane, Lieut. G. P. ; Mitchell, Lieut. G. D. ; Mott, Major J. E. ; Potts, Lieut. R. E. (with bar); Arnold, Lieut. T. F. ; Brown, Lieut. W. J. ; Cameron, Lieut. R. E. ; Carter, Capt. L. L. ; Cumming, Capt. D. G. (with bar); Devine, Chaplain W. (attached) ; Downes, Lieut. H. ; Gelston, Lieut. A. J. ; Henderson, Lieut. G. K.; King, Capt. C. H.; McDowall, Lieut. M. B.; Morley, Lieut. T.; Moyes, Major A. G.; Reid, Lieut. R. B.; Stoerkel, Lieut. C. W. (with bar); Stabback, Lieut. J. W. ; Sheperdson, Lieut. H. M. ; Twining, Capt. D. A. ; True, Capt. E. (attached).

D.C.M.:—Arnold, L.-Cpl. T. F. (Lieut.) ; Baker, R.S.M. A. K. ; Clunes, Pte. D. ; Davies, Sergt. T. O. ; Jones, Cpl. H. E. ; Kirkpatrick, Pte. R. L. ; Lawson, Cpl. S. R. ; Price, Cpl. T. A. ; Smith, L.-Cpl. P. ; Tognini, Pte. C. ; Thomas, L.-Cpl. W. H. ; Yates, Pte. A. V. ; Borrie, Pte. R. E. ; Corr, Cpl. W. B. (Lieut.) ; Davies, Sergt. H. D. ; Garland, C.S.M. H. G. ; Kearey, Pte. R. G. ; Kingston, Sergt. A. L. (Lieut.) ; Mitchell, L.-Cpl. G. D. (Lieut.) ; Symes, Sergt. P. ; Schocroft, L.-Cpl. C. S. ; Tregoweth, Pte. F. G. A. ; Wells, Pte. R. G.

Military Medal :—Abrahall, Pte. J. H. ; Adams, L.-Cpl. J. ; Alcorn, Sergt. C. H. (with bar); Arnold, L.-Cpl. T. F. (Lieut.); Bradford, Pte. J. ; Bray, Pte. R. W. ; Brown, Pte. E. F. ; Brown, Pte. E. S. ; Brown, Lieut. W. J. (with bar); Burton, Sergt. S. M. ; Byron, Pte. J. W. ; Bailey, Pte. T. A. ; Bambridge, Pte. H. S. ; Baker, L.-Cpl. J. T. ; Beaton, Sergt. E. ; Bennett, Dvr. J. F. ; Bentley, Pte. E. ; Bing, Pte. W.; Bockelberg, A.-Cpl. W.; Bonython, Cpl. G. G. (Lieut.) ; Boucher, Pte. J. W. ; Boylan, Pte. T. ; Barrow, Pte. S. J. ; Binnie, L.-Cpl. J. M. ; Bobridge, Sergt. E. A. ; Carr, Cpl. A. F. ; Carter, Pte. A. J. ; Chew, L.-Cpl. J. H. ; Cleggert, Pte. R. ; Condron, L.-Cpl. T. ; Connaughton, L.-Cpl. W. J. ; Crebert, Pte. K. J. ; Conlan, Sergt. P. ; Dawson, Pte. G. E. ; Davoren, Pte. H. J. ; Day, Pte. W. W. ; Dennis, Sergt. E. J. ; Dick, Sergt. G. ; Dimond, Pte. C. L. ; Donovan, Pte. P. (with bar); Duck, Pte. R. ; Daly, Cpl. G. ; Davies, Pte. T. W. ; Davies, Pte. J. P.; Downes, Sergt. H. (Lieut.); Egan, L.-Cpl. H. J. W.; Evans, Sergt. D. ; Fennell, L.-Cpl. J. ; Fisher, L.-Cpl. D. H. ; Farnden, Pte. A. J. ; Ford, L.-Cpl. A. P. (Lieut.) ; Fraser, Pte. J. G. ; Gibson, Cpl. K. E. (with bar); Gibson, Sergt. T. ; Gunner, Sergt. H. ; Gwiney, Pte. J. J. ; Haigh, Pte. J. F. ; Hall, Pte. J. ; Halliday, Sergt. E. A. ;

BATTALION'S HONOURS AND AWARDS.

Hammond, Sergt. T. W.; Henderson, Sergt. G. K. (Lieut.); Hodges, L.-Cpl. T. B.; Hogan, Pte. J. G. (with bar); Irvine, Pte. J. L.; Jarvis, Pte. K. G.; Jeffery, Pte. A.; Jeffs, Pte. H. R.; Jell, Pte. C.; Jones, L.-Cpl. H. E.; Juers, Pte. A. H.; Kealy, Sergt. R. J.; Keep, Pte. R. S.; King, Pte. C. A.; Kirwan, Sergt. S. J.; Klemettilla, Pte. A.; Kamprod, L.-Cpl. F. J.; Lane, L.-Cpl. W. H.; Langdon, Pte. W. Y. (with bar); Letpbridge, Pte. E. M.; Lewis, Cpl. J. A.; Lindner, L.-Cpl. L. M.; Lloyd, L.-Cpl. R. J.; Lord, Pte. H.; Lovell, Pte. G. W.; Loyton, Cpl. T. S.; Luetchford, Sergt. D. F.; Lines, Pte. A. G.; Millhouse, Pte. J. H.; Morris, Pte. F.; Massey, Sergt. S.; Middleton, Pte. A. W.; McDonald, Pte. H.; Mumme, Cpl. H. J.; McAdam, Pte. G. M.; McArthur, Sergt. T. A.; McConnell, Pte. H. J.; McDougall, Sergt. S. R.; McDowall, Lieut. M. B. T.; McGrath, Cpl. J. J.; McInerney, Pte. J.; McKenzie, Driver F.; McCrae, Cpl. J.; Marks, Pte. H. E.; Marron, Pte. O. J.; Marsh, L.-Cpl. J. C.; Mason, Pte. J. W. H.; Mason, Pte. O. G.; Maynard, Cpl. H. H.; Nielsen, Pte. H. K.; Nicholson, L.-Cpl. E.; O'Brien, Sergt. M. P.; O'Loughlin, Pte. E. F.; O'Neill, Pte. E.; O'Neill, Cpl. G. D.; O'Neill, Pte. W. R. (with bar); Onions, Pte. B. L. (with bar); Pettingill, Pte. H. J.; Pitt, Cpl. J.; Pitt, Coms. C. C.; Polkinghorne, Sergt. J. G.; Pope, Pte. W.; Price, Cpl. A.; Price, L.-Cpl. H. T.; Patterson, L.-Cpl. W. J. H.; Payne, Sergt. J. C.; Pengelly, Pte. W. P.; Quinlan, Pte. J. A.; Rafferty, Sergt. R. S.; Ratpke, Cpl. H. O.; Rickard, Pte. J. J.; Robbins, Sergt. L. T. F.; Roberts, Pte. B. H. R.; Robinson, Pte. R. J.; Roe, Sergt. A. A.; Rochford, L.-Cpl. J.; Schramm, Pte. F. L.; Stribley, Pte. W. H.; Stuart, Cpl. W. G. R.; Seal, Sergt. G. C.; Sheperdson, 2nd-Lieut. H. M.; Slater, L.-Cpl. J. G. V.; Small, Pte. W. C.; Sawyer, Pte. H. J.; Scaresbrook, Pte. J.; Schammer, L.-Cpl. A. E.; Schocroft, L.-Cpl. C. S.; Talbot, Pte. H. A.; Thomas, Pte. W. J.; Ticklie, Pte. A. T.; Tornquist, L.-Cpl. F. W.; Tuame, Pte. O.; Twining, Sergt. D. A. (Capt.) (pres. Capt.); Woods, L.-Cpl. B. L.; Woods, L.-Cpl. Wm.; Wright, Pte. L. N. J. (with bar); Weaver, L.-Cpl. R.; Webb, L.-Cpl. W. L.; Weir, Cpl. T.; Wharton, Pte. W. M.; Whyte, Pte. C. Stephens; Wilkinson, Pte. A. H.; Williams, Pte. E. T.; Williams, Pte. W. H.; Williamson, Pte. A.; Wall, Pte. J. T. (with bar); Wardell-Johnson, Pte. P. L.

M.S.M. :—Cornish, Sergt. A. H.; Crudace, Sergt. A. L.; Kingston, Sergt. A. C. W.

Foreign Decorations :

Croix de Guerre (French) :— Devine, Chaplain W. (attached); Douglas, Sergt. E.; Leane, Lieut.-Col. R. L.; Lindsay, Capt. D. E.; Middleton, Driver W.; Twining, Capt. D. A.; Raferty, Pte. J. L.; Woollard, Major H. H. (attached).

Croix de Guerre (Belgian) :—Howells, Cpl. S. W.

Servian :—Leane, Major B. B.

Russian Medal :—Stabback, Lieut. J. W.

MELBOURNE:
M'CARRON, BIRD AND CO., PRINTERS,
479 COLLINS STREET.